THE
POWER
IN
PRAYER

THE
POWER
IN
PRAYER

Charles Spurgeon

Whitaker House

All Scripture quotations are from the *King James Version* (KJV) of the Bible.

THE POWER IN PRAYER

ISBN: 0-88368-441-1
Printed in the United States of America
Copyright © 1996 by Whitaker House

Whitaker House
30 Hunt Valley Circle
New Kensington, PA 15068

4 5 6 7 8 9 10 11 / 06 05 04 03 02 01 00 99 98

Contents

Chapter One

Guaranteed to Succeed

And I say unto you, Ask, and it shall be given you; seek, and ye shall find; knock, and it shall be opened unto you. For every one that asketh receiveth; and he that seeketh findeth; and to him that knocketh it shall be opened.
—Luke 11:9–10

To seek aid in time of distress from a supernatural being is an instinct of human nature. I do not mean that human nature unrenewed ever offers truly spiritual prayer or ever exercises saving faith in the living God. But still, like a child crying in the dark, with painful longing for help from somewhere or other, the soul in deep sorrow almost always cries to some supernatural being for help. None have been more ready to pray in time of trouble than those who have ridiculed prayer in their prosperity. In fact, probably no prayers have been truer to the feelings of the hour than those that atheists have offered when in fear of death.

In one of his papers in the *Tattler,* Addison describes a man who, on board ship, loudly boasted of his atheism. A brisk gale springing up, he fell on his knees and confessed to the chaplain that he had been an atheist. The common seamen, who had never heard the word before, thought it was some strange fish. They were more surprised when they saw it was a man and learned out of his own mouth that he never believed until that day that there was a God. One of the old sailors whispered to an officer that it would be a good deed to heave him overboard, but this was a cruel suggestion, for the poor creature was already in misery enough. His atheism had evaporated, and in mortal terror he cried to God to have mercy on him.

Similar incidents have occurred more than once or twice. Indeed, so frequently does boastful skepticism tumble down at the end that we always expect it to do so. Take away unnatural restraint from the mind, and it may be said of all men that, like the comrades of Jonah, they cry *"every man unto his god"* (Jonah 1:5) in their trouble. As birds to their nests and as deer to their hiding places, so men in agony fly to a superior being for help in the hour of need.

By instinct man turned to his God in Paradise. Now, though he is to a sad degree a dethroned monarch, there lingers in his memory shadows of what he was and remembrances of where his strength must still be found. Therefore, no matter where you find a man, you will meet one who will ask for supernatural help in his distress.

I believe in the truthfulness of this instinct, and I believe that man prays because there is something in prayer. When the Creator gives His creature the power of thirst, it is because water exists to meet its thirst. When He creates hunger, there is food to correspond to the appetite. Even so, when He inclines men to pray, it is because prayer has a corresponding blessing connected with it.

We find a powerful reason for expecting prayer to be effective in the fact that it is an institution of God. In God's Word we are over and over again commanded to pray. God's institutions are not folly. Can I believe that the infinitely wise God has ordained for me an exercise that is ineffective and is no more than child's play? Does He tell me to pray, and yet does prayer have no more of a result than if I whistled to the wind or sang to a grove of trees? If there is no answer to prayer, prayer is a monstrous absurdity, and God is the author of it, which it is blasphemy to assert. Only a fool will continue to pray when you have once proved to him that prayer has no effect with God and never receives an answer. If it is indeed true that its effects end with the man who prays, prayer is a work for idiots and madmen, not for sane people!

I will not enter into any arguments upon the matter. Rather, I am coming to my text, which to me, at least, and to you who are followers of Christ, is the end of all controversy. Our Savior knew quite well that many difficulties would arise in connection with prayer that might tend to stagger His disciples, and therefore He has balanced every opposition by an overwhelming assurance. Read those words, *"I say unto you."* *"I"*—your Teacher, your Master, your Lord, your Savior, your God—*"I say unto you, Ask, and it shall be given you; seek, and ye shall find; knock, and it shall be opened unto you."*

In the text our Lord meets all difficulties first by giving us the weight of His own authority: *"I say unto you."* Next, He presents us with a promise: *"Ask, and it shall be given you"* and so on. Then He reminds us of an indisputable fact: *"Every one that asketh receiveth."* Here are three mortal wounds for a Christian's doubts about prayer.

His Authority

First, then, our Savior gives to us the weight of His own authority: *"I say unto you."* The first mark of a follower of Christ is that he believes his Lord. We do not follow the Lord at all if we raise any questions on points about which He speaks explicitly. Even if a doctrine is surrounded by ten thousand difficulties, the *ipse dixit* of the Lord Jesus sweeps them all away, so far as true Christians are concerned. Our Master's declaration is all the argument we want. *"I say unto you"* is our logic. Reason, we see you at your best in Jesus, for He is made wisdom to us by God (1 Cor. 1:30). He cannot err; He cannot lie; if He says, *"I say unto you,"* there is an end of all debate.

However, there are certain reasons that should lead us to rest all the more confidently in our Master's word upon this point. There is power in every word of the Lord Jesus, but there is special force in the utterance before us. It has been objected about prayer that it is not possible for prayer to be answered because the laws of nature are unalterable and they must and will go on whether men pray or not. To us it does not seem necessary to prove that the laws of nature are disturbed. God can work miracles, and He may work them yet again as

He has done in times long past. However, it is no part of the Christian faith that God must work miracles in order to answer the prayers of His servants. When a man has to disarrange all his affairs and, so to speak, stop all his machinery in order to fulfill a promise, it proves that he is but a man and that his wisdom and power are limited. But He is God indeed who, without reversing the engine or removing a single cog from a wheel, fulfills the desires of His people as they come up before Him. The Lord is so omnipotent that He can work results tantamount to miracles without in the slightest degree suspending any one of His laws. In olden times He did, as it were, stop the machinery of the universe to answer a prayer (see Joshua 10:12–13), but now, with equally godlike glory, He orders events so as to answer believing prayers and yet suspends no natural law.

But this is far from being our only or our main comfort. Our main comfort is that we hear the voice of One who is competent to speak on the matter, and He says, *"I say unto you, Ask, and it shall be given you."* Whether the laws of nature are reversible or irreversible, *"Ask, and it shall be given you; seek, and ye shall find."* Now, who is He that speaks this way? It is He who made all things, without whom *"was not any thing made that was made"* (John 1:3). Can He not speak on this point? Eternal Word, who *"was in the beginning with God"* (John 1:2), balancing the clouds and fastening the foundations of the earth, You know what the laws and the unalterable constitutions of nature may be. If You say, *"Ask, and it shall be given you,"* then assuredly it will be so, be the laws of nature what they may.

Besides, our Lord is the sustainer of all things. Seeing that all the laws of nature operate only through His power and are sustained by His might, He must be aware of the motion of all the forces in the world. Therefore, if He says, *"Ask, and it shall be given you,"* He does not speak in ignorance, but He knows what He affirms. We may be assured that there are no forces that can prevent the fulfillment of the Lord's own word. From the Creator and the Sustainer, the word *"I say unto you"* settles all controversy forever.

Another objection has been raised that is very ancient indeed, and it has a great appearance of force. It is raised not so much by skeptics as by those who hold a part of the truth. It is this: prayer can certainly produce no results because the decrees of God have settled everything and those decrees are immutable. Now, we have no desire to deny the assertion that the decrees of God have settled all events. Certainly, it is our full belief that God has foreknown and predestinated everything that happens in heaven above or in the earth beneath. I fully believe that the foreknown station of a reed by the river is as fixed as the station of a king, and the chaff from the hand of the winnower is steered as the stars in their courses. Predestination embraces the great and the little; it reaches to all things. The question is, Why pray? Might it not as logically be asked, Why breathe, eat, move, or do anything? We have an answer that satisfies us; namely, our prayers are in the predestination, and God has as much ordained His people's prayers as anything else. So, when we pray, we are producing links in the chain of ordained facts. Destiny decrees that I should pray—I pray. Destiny decrees that I will be answered—the answer comes to me.

But we have a better answer than all this. Our Lord Jesus Christ comes forward, and He says to us, "My dear children, the decrees of God need not trouble you; there is nothing in them inconsistent with your prayers being heard. *'I say unto you, Ask, and it shall be given you.'"*

Now, who is the One who that says this? Why, it is He who has been with the Father from the beginning: *"The same was in the beginning with God"* (John 1:2). He knows what the purposes of the Father are and what the heart of the Father is, for He has told us in another place, *"The Father himself loveth you"* (John 16:27). Now, since He knows the decrees of the Father and the heart of the Father, He can tell us with the absolute certainty of an eyewitness that there is nothing in the eternal purposes in conflict with this truth, that he who asks receives and he who seeks finds. He has read the decrees from beginning to end. Has He not taken the book, loosed the seven seals thereof (Rev. 5:5), and declared the ordinances of heaven? He tells you there is nothing there inconsistent with your bended knee and streaming eye and with the Father's opening the windows of heaven to shower upon you the blessings that you seek.

Moreover, the One who promises to answer prayer is God Himself. The purposes of heaven are His own purposes. He who ordained the purpose here gives the assurance that there is nothing in it to prevent the efficacy of prayer. *"I say unto you."* You who believe in Him, your doubts are scattered to the winds; you know that He hears prayer.

But sometimes there arises in our minds another difficulty, which is associated with our own judgment of ourselves and our estimate of God. We feel that God is very great, and we tremble in the presence of His majesty. We feel that we are very little and that we are also vile. It does seem an incredible thing that such guilty nothings should have power to move the arm that moves the world. I am not surprised if that fear often hampers us in prayer. But Jesus answers it so sweetly. He says, *"I say unto you, Ask, and it shall be given you."*

I ask again, Who is it that says, *"I say unto you"*? Why, it is He who knows both the greatness of God and the weakness of man. He is God, and out of His excellent majesty I think I hear Him say, *"I say unto you, Ask, and it shall be given you."* But He is also man like ourselves, and He says, "Do not dread your littleness, for I, bone of your bone and flesh of your flesh, assure you that God hears man's prayer."

Again, if the dread of sin should haunt us and our own sorrow depress us, I would remind you that Jesus Christ, when He says, *"I say unto you,"* gives us the authority, not only of His person, but of His experience. Jesus prayed. Never did any pray as He did. Nights were spent in prayer by Him and whole days in earnest intercession, and He says to us, *"I say unto you, Ask, and it shall be given you."* I think I see Him coming fresh from the heather of the hills, among which He had knelt all night to pray, and He says, "My disciples, *'Ask, and it shall be given you';* for I have prayed, and it has been given to me." He *"was heard in that he feared"* (Heb. 5:7), and therefore He says to us, *"I say unto you...knock, and it shall be opened unto you."* I think I hear Him speak thus from the cross, His face bright with the first beam of sunlight after He had borne *"our sins in his own body on the tree"* (1 Pet. 2:24) and had suffered all our griefs to the last pang. He had cried, *"My God, my God, why hast thou forsaken me?"* (Matt. 27:46); now, having received an answer, He cries in triumph, *"It is finished"* (John 19:30). In so doing, He bids us also to *"ask, and it shall be given* [us]." Jesus has proved the power of prayer.

Remember, too, that if Jesus our Lord could speak so positively here, there is an even greater reason for believing Him now: He has gone within the veil, and He sits at the right hand of God, even the Father. (See Hebrews 6:19–20; 10:12.) The voice does not come to us from the man of poverty, wearing a garment without seam, but from the enthroned priest with the golden girdle about His loins. It is He who now says, from the right hand of God, *"I say unto you, Ask, and it shall be given you."*

Do you not believe in His name? How then can a prayer that is sincerely offered in that name fall to the ground? When you present your petition in Jesus' name (John 15:16; 16:23), a part of His authority clothes your prayers. If your prayer is rejected, Christ is dishonored; you cannot believe that. You have trusted Him; then believe that prayer offered through Him must and will win the day.

We cannot stay any longer on this point, but we trust the Holy Spirit will impress it upon your heart.

His Promise

We will now remember that our Lord presents us with a promise. Note that the promise is given to several varieties of prayer. *"I say unto you, Ask, and it shall be given you; seek, and ye shall find; knock, and it shall be opened unto you."* The text clearly asserts that all forms of true prayer will be heard, provided they are presented through Jesus Christ and are for promised blessings. Some are vocal prayers: men ask aloud. Never should we fail to offer up every day continually the prayer that is uttered by the tongue, for the promise is that the asker will be heard. But there are others who, not neglecting vocal prayer, are far more abundant in active prayer. By humble and diligent use of the means, they seek for the blessings that they need. Their heart speaks to God by its longings, strivings, emotions, and labors. Let them not cease seeking, for they will surely find. There are others who, in their earnestness, combine the most eager forms, both acting and speaking, for knocking is a loud kind of asking and a vehement form of seeking.

So the prayers grow from asking, which is the statement, to seeking, which is the pleading, and then to knocking, which is the urgent requesting. To each of these stages of prayer there is a distinct promise. He who asks will have; what more did he ask for? But he who seeks will go further; he will find, will enjoy, will grasp, and will know that he has obtained. He who knocks will go further still, for he will understand, and to him will the precious thing be opened. He will not merely have the blessing and enjoy it, but he will comprehend it. He will *comprehend with all saints what is the ...depth, and height*" (Eph. 3:18).

I want you, however, to notice this fact, which covers all: whatever form your prayer may assume, it will succeed. If you only ask, you will receive. If you seek, you will find. If you knock, it will be opened. In each case, *"according to your faith* [will it be] *unto you"* (Matt. 9:29). The clauses of the promise before us are not put, as we say in law, jointly: he that asks and seeks and knocks will receive. They are put separately: he that asks will have; he that seeks will find; he that knocks will have it opened. It is not when we combine all three that we get the blessing, though, doubtless, if we did combine them, we would get the combined reply. But if we exercise only one of these three forms of prayer, we will still get that which our souls seek after.

These three methods of prayer exercise a variety of our graces. It is a gloss of the forefathers upon this passage that faith asks, hope seeks, and love knocks, and the gloss is worth repeating. Faith asks because it believes God will give. Hope, having asked, expects and therefore seeks for the blessing. Love comes nearer still; it will not take a denial from God but desires to enter into His house and to dine with Him. Therefore, love knocks at His door until He opens.

But, again, let us come back to the old point. It does not matter which grace is exercised; a blessing comes to each one. If faith asks, it will receive; if hope seeks, it will find; and if love knocks, it will be opened to it.

These three modes of prayer suit us in different stages of distress. There I am, a poor beggar at mercy's door; I ask, and I will receive. But suppose I lose my way so that I cannot find Him of whom I once asked so successfully. Well, then I may seek with the certainty that I will find. And if I am in the last stage of all, not merely poor and bewildered, but so defiled that I feel shut out from God, like a leper shut out of the camp, then I may knock and the door will open to me.

Each one of these different descriptions of prayer is exceedingly simple. If anybody said, "I cannot ask," our reply would be, "You do not understand the word." Surely everybody can ask. A little child can ask. Long before an infant can speak, he can ask; he does not need to use words in order to ask for what he wants. Not one among us is incapacitated from asking. Prayers need not be fine. I believe God abhors fine prayers. When we pray, the simpler our prayers are, the better. The plainest, humblest language that expresses our meaning is the best.

The next word is *seek,* and surely there is no difficulty about seeking. In finding there might be, but in seeking there is none. When the woman in the parable lost her money, she lit a candle and sought for it. I do not suppose that she had ever been to a university, that she qualified as a lady physician, or that she could have sat on a school board as a woman of superior intellect, but she could seek. Anybody who desires to do so can seek, whether man, woman, or child. For their encouragement the promise is not given to some particular philosophical form of seeking, but *"he that seeketh findeth."*

Then there is knocking. Well, that is a thing of no great difficulty. We used to do it when we were boys, sometimes too much for the neighbors' comfort. And at home, if the knocker was a little too high, we had ways and means of knocking at the door even then. A stone would do it, or the heel of a boot would do it. Anything would make a knock. It was not beyond our capacity by any means. Therefore, it is put in this fashion by Christ Himself, as much as to tell us, "You do not need to have scholarship, training, talent, or wit for prayer. Ask, seek, knock—that is all. And the promise is to every one of these ways of praying."

Will you believe the promise? It is Christ who gives it. No lie ever fell from His lips. Oh, doubt Him not. Pray on if you have prayed, and if you have never prayed before, may God help you to begin today!

His Testimony

Our third point is that Jesus testifies to the fact that prayer is heard. Having given a promise, He then adds, in effect: "You may be quite sure that this promise will be fulfilled, not only because I say it, but because it is and always has been so." When a man says the sun will rise tomorrow morning, we believe it because it always has risen. Our Lord tells us an indisputable fact: all through the ages true asking has been followed by receiving. Remember that He who stated this fact knew it. If you state a fact, you may say, "Yes, as far as my observation goes, it is true." But the observation of Christ was unbounded. There was never a true prayer offered unknown to Him. Prayers acceptable with the Most High come up to Him by the way of the wounds of Christ. Hence, the Lord Jesus Christ can speak by personal knowledge, and His declaration is that prayer is successful. *"Every one that asketh receiveth; and he that seeketh findeth."*

Now, here we must, of course, accept the limitations that would be made by ordinary common sense and that are made by Scripture. It is not everyone who frivolously or wickedly asks or pretends to ask of God that gets what he asks for. It is not every silly, idle, unconsidered request of unregenerate hearts that God will answer. By no means. Common sense limits the statement so far. Besides, Scripture limits it again. *"Ye have not, because ye ask not...* [or] *because ye ask amiss"* (James 4:2–3). There is an asking amiss which will never obtain. But those things being remembered, the statement of our Lord has no other qualification: *"Every one that asketh receiveth."*

Let it be remembered that frequently even when the ungodly and the wicked have asked of God, they have received. Often in the times of distress, they have called upon God, and He has answered them. "Do you really say so?" asks one. No, I do not say so, but the Scripture says so. Ahab's prayer was answered, and the Lord said,

> *Seest thou how Ahab humbleth himself before me? because he humbleth himself before me, I will not bring the evil in his days: but in his son's days will I bring the evil upon his house.* (1 Kings 21:29)

So, also, the Lord heard the prayer of Jehoahaz, the son of Jehu, who did evil in the sight of the Lord. (See 2 Kings 13:1–4.) When the Israelites were given over to their foes because of their sins, they cried to God for deliverance, and they were answered. Yet the Lord Himself testified concerning them that they only flattered with their mouths (Ps. 78:34–36).

Does this surprise you? Does He not hear the young ravens when they cry? Do you think He will not hear man, who is formed in His own image? Do you doubt it? Remember Nineveh. (See Jonah 3:1–10.) The prayers offered at Nineveh, were they spiritual prayers? Did you ever hear of a church of God in Nineveh? I have not; neither do I believe the Ninevites were ever visited by converting grace. They were, however, convinced by the preaching of Jonah that they were in danger from the great Jehovah. They proclaimed a fast and humbled themselves, God heard their prayer, and Nineveh for a while was preserved.

Many times in the hour of sickness and in the time of woe, God has heard the prayers of the unthankful and the evil. Do you think God gives nothing except to the good? Have you dwelled at the foot of Sinai and learned to judge according to the law of merit? What were you when you began to pray? Were you good and righteous? Has not God commanded you to do good to the evil? (See Matthew 5:44.) Will He command you to do what He will not do Himself? Has He not said that He *sendeth rain on the just and on the unjust"* (Matt.

5:45), and is it not so? Is He not daily blessing those who curse Him and doing good to those who despitefully use Him? This is one of the glories of God's grace. When there is nothing else good in the man, yet if there is a cry lifted up from his heart, the Lord condescends to send relief from trouble. Now, if God has heard the prayers even of men who have not sought Him in the highest manner and has given them temporary deliverances in answer to their cries, will He not much more hear you when you are humbling yourself in His sight and desiring to be reconciled to Him? Surely you can use this as an argument that God will answer your prayers.

But to come more fully to the point with regard to real and spiritual prayers, *"Every one that asketh receiveth"* without any limit whatsoever. There has never been an instance yet of a man really seeking spiritual blessings from God without his receiving them. The tax collector stood afar off, and so broken was his heart that he dared not look up to heaven, yet God looked down on him. (See Luke 18:13–14.) Manasseh lay in the low dungeon. He had been a cruel persecutor of the saints. There was nothing in him that could commend him to God. But God heard him out of the dungeon and brought him forth to liberty of soul. (See 2

Chronicles 33:1–13.) Jonah had by his own sin brought himself into the whale's belly, and he was an irritable servant of God at best. But out of the belly of hell he cried, and God heard him. (See Jonah 1:17–2:2.) *"Every one that asketh receiveth; and he that seeketh findeth; and to him that knocketh it shall be opened."* Everyone. If I needed evidence, I should be able to find it among believers. I would ask any follower of Christ to bear witness that God heard his prayer. I do not believe that among the damned in hell there is one who would dare say, "I sought the Lord, and He rejected me."

There will not be found at the last day of account one single soul that can say, "I knocked at mercy's door, but God refused to open it." There will not stand before the Great White Throne a single soul that can plead, "O Christ, I would have been saved by You, but You would not save me. I gave myself up into Your hands, but You rejected me. I penitently asked You for mercy, but You did not give it." *"Every one that asketh receiveth."* It has been so until this day; it will be so until Christ Himself will come. If you doubt it, try it; if you have tried it, try it again.

Are you in rags? That does not matter— *"Every one that asketh receiveth."* Are you foul with sin? That means nothing—*"He that seeketh findeth."* Do you feel as if you were shut out from God altogether? That does not matter either—*"Knock, and it shall be opened unto you. For every one that asketh receiveth."*

Is there no election there? Doubtless there is, but that does not alter this truth that has no limit to it whatsoever—*"every one."* What a rich text it is! *"Every one that asketh receiveth."*

When our Lord spoke this, He could have pointed to His own life as evidence. At any rate, we can refer to it now and show that there is no one who asked of Christ who did not receive. The Syrophenician woman was at first repulsed when the Lord called her a dog, but when she had the courage to say, *"Yet the dogs eat of the crumbs which fall from their masters' table"* (Matt. 15:27), she soon discovered that *"every one that asketh receiveth."* She, also, who came behind Him in the crowd and touched the hem of His garment, was no asker, but she was a seeker, and she found. (See Matthew 9:20–22.)

I think I hear, in answer to all this, the lamentable wail of one who says, "I have been crying to God a long time for salvation. I have asked, I have sought, and I have knocked, but it has not come yet." Well, dear friend, if I am asked who is true, God or you, I know whom I will stand by, and I would advise you to believe God before you believe yourself. God will hear prayer, but do you know there is one thing before prayer? What is it? Why, the Gospel is not "he who prays will be saved." That is not the Gospel. I believe he will be saved, but that is not the Gospel that I am told to preach to you. *"Go ye into all the world, and preach the gospel to every creature. He"*—what?—*"He that believeth and is baptized shall be saved"* (Mark 16:15–16).

Now, you have been asking God to save you. Do you expect Him to save you without your believing and being baptized? Surely you have not had the impudence to ask God to make void His own word! Might He not say to you, "Do as I tell you; believe My Son. He that believes on Him has everlasting life"? (See John 3:16.) Let me ask you, Do you believe Jesus Christ? Will you trust Him? "Oh, I trust Him," says one. "I trust Him wholly." Soul, do not ask for salvation anymore. You have it already; you are saved. If you trust Jesus with all your soul, your sins are forgiven, and you are saved. The next time you approach the Lord, go with praise as well as with prayer, and sing and bless His name.

"But how do I know that I am saved?" asks one. God says, *"He that believeth and is baptized shall be saved"* (Mark 16:16). Have you believed? Have you been baptized? If so, you are saved. How do I know that? On the best evidence in all the world: God says you are. Do you want any evidence besides that? "I want to feel it." Feel! Are your feelings better than God's witness? Will you make God a liar by asking more signs and tokens than His sure word of testimony? I have no evidence this day that I dare trust in concerning my salvation but this, that I rest on Christ alone with all my heart and soul and strength. Other refuge have I none. If you have that evidence, it is all the evidence that you need to seek for this day. Other witnesses of grace in your heart will come by and by and cluster around you and adorn the doctrine you profess, but now your first business is to believe in Jesus.

"I have asked for faith," says one. Well, what do you mean by that? To believe in Jesus Christ is the gift of God, but it must be your own act as well. Do you think God will believe for you or that the Holy Spirit believes instead of you? What does the Holy Spirit have to believe? You must believe for yourself or be lost. He cannot lie; will you not believe in Him? He deserves to be believed. Trust in Him, and you are saved, and your prayer is answered.

I think I hear another say, "I trust that I am already saved, but I have been looking for the salvation of others in answer to my prayers." Dear friend, you will get it. *"Every one that asketh receiveth; and he that seeketh findeth; and to him that knocketh it shall be opened."* "But I have sought the conversion of a certain person for years with many prayers." You will have it, or you will know one day why you do not have it and will be made content not to have it.

Pray on in hope. Many a one has had his prayer for others answered after he had been dead. There was a father who had prayed for many years for his sons and daughters, and yet they were not converted but became exceedingly worldly. His time came to die. He gathered his children around his bed, hoping to bear such a witness for Christ at the end that it might be blessed to their conversion. But, unhappily for him, he was in deep distress of soul; he had doubts about his own interest in Christ. He was one of God's children who are put to bed in the dark. This was, above all, the worst fear of his mind, that his dear children would see his distress and be prejudiced against religion. The good man was buried, his sons came to the funeral, and God heard the man's prayer that very day. For as they went away from the grave, one of them said to the other, "Brother, our father died a most unhappy death."

"He did, brother. I was very astonished at it, for I never knew a better man than our father."

"Ah," said the first brother, "if a holy man such as our father found it a hard thing to die, it will be a dreadful thing for us who have no faith when our time comes." That same thought had struck them all and drove them to the cross, and so the good man's prayer was heard in a mysterious way.

Heaven and earth will pass away, but while God lives, prayer must be heard. While God remains true to His word, supplication is not in vain. May the Lord give you grace to exercise it continually. Amen.

Chapter Two

The Raven's Cry

He giveth to the beast his food,
and to the young ravens which cry.
—Psalm 147:9

I will open this chapter with a quotation. I must give you in Caryl's own words his note on ravens.

Naturalists tell us, that when the raven hath fed his young in the nest till they are well fledged and able to fly abroad, then he thrusts them out of the nest, and will not let them abide there, but puts them to get their own living. Now when these young ones are upon their first flight from their nest, and are little acquainted with means how to help themselves with food, then the Lord provides food for them.

It is said by credible authorities, that the raven is marvellous strict and severe in this; for as soon as his young ones are able to provide for themselves, he will not fetch any more food for them; yea, some affirm, the old ones will not suffer them to stay in the same country where they were bred; and if so, then they must needs wander.

We say proverbially, "Need makes the old wife trot"; we may say, and "the young ones, too." It hath been, and possibly is, the practice of some parents towards their children, who, as soon as they can shift for themselves, and are fit in any competency to get their bread, they turn them out of doors, as the raven doth his young ones out of the nest.

Now, saith the Lord in the text, when the young ones of the raven are at this pinch, that they are turned off, and wander for lack of meat, who then provides for them? Do not I, the Lord? Do not I, who provide for the old raven, provide for his young ones, both while they abide in the nest and when they wander for lack of meat?

Solomon sent the sluggard to the ant, and he himself learned lessons from badgers, greyhounds, and spiders. Let us be willing to be instructed by any of God's creatures. Let us go to the raven's nest now to learn as in a school.

Our blessed Lord once derived a very potent argument from ravens, an argument intended to comfort and cheer those of His servants who were oppressed with needless anxieties about their temporal circumstances. To such He said,

> *Consider the ravens: for they neither sow nor reap; which neither have storehouse nor barn; and God feedeth them: how much more are ye better than the fowls?*
> (Luke 12:24)

Following the Master's logic, I will argue here in this manner: Consider the ravens as they cry. With harsh, inarticulate, croaking notes they make known their wants, and your heavenly Father answers their prayer and sends them food. You, too, have begun to pray and to seek His favor. Are you not much better than they? Does God care for ravens, and will He not care for you? Does He listen to the cries of the unfledged ravens in their nests when they cry to Him in their hunger and watch to be fed? Does He, I say, supply them in answer to their cries, and will He not answer you, poor, trembling children of men who are seeking His face and favor through Jesus Christ?

The whole business of this chapter will simply be to work out that one thought. I will aim, under the guidance of the Holy Spirit, to write something to those who have been praying for mercy but as yet have not received it; who have gone on their knees, perhaps for months, with one exceeding great and bitter cry but as yet know not the way of peace. Their sin still hangs like a millstone around their necks; they sit in the valley of the shadow of death; no light has dawned upon them; and they are wringing their hands and moaning, "Has God forgotten to be gracious? Has He shut His ear against the prayers of seeking souls? Will He be mindful of sinners' piteous cries no more? Will penitents' tears drop upon the earth and no longer move His compassion?"

Satan, too, is telling you, dear friends who are now in this state of mind, that God will never hear you, that He will let you cry until you die, that you will pant out your life in sighs and tears, and that at the end you will be cast into the lake of fire.

I long to give you some comfort and encouragement. I want to urge you to cry yet more vehemently, to come to the cross and lay hold of it and vow that you will never leave its shadow until you find the blessing that your soul covets. I want to move you, if God the Holy Spirit will help me, so that you will say within yourselves, like Queen Esther, *"I [will] go in unto the king...and if I perish, I perish"* (Est. 4:16). May you add to that the vow of Jacob, *"I will not let thee go, except thou bless me!"* (Gen. 32:26).

More Valuable Than a Raven

Here, then, is the question at hand, Since God hears the young ravens, will He not hear you? First, I argue that He will when I remember that it is only a raven that cries and that you, in some senses, are much better than a raven. The raven is only a poor, unclean bird, whose instant death would make no grievous gap in creation. If thousands of ravens had their necks wrung tomorrow, I do not think that there would be any vehement grief and sorrow in the universe about them. There would simply be a number of poor dead birds, and that would be all.

You, however, are an immortal soul. The raven is gone when life is over; there is no raven any longer. But when your present life is past, you have not ceased to be; you are launched upon the sea of life; you have begun to live forever. You will see earth's ancient mountains crumble to nothingness before your immortal spirit will expire. The moon will have paled her feeble light, and the sun's more mighty fires will have been quenched in perpetual darkness. Yet, your spirit will still be marching on in its everlasting course—an everlasting course of misery unless God hears your cry.

> Oh, that truth immense,
> This mortal, immortality shall wear!
> The pulse of mind shall never cease to play;
> By God awakened, it forever throbs,
> Eternal as His own eternity!
> Above the angels, or below the fields:
> To mount in glory, or in shame descend—
> Mankind are destined by resistless doom.

Do you think, then, that God will hear the poor bird that exists and exists not, that is here a moment and then blotted out of existence, and will He not hear you, an immortal soul, whose duration is to be coequal with His own? I think it surely must strike you that if He hears the dying raven, He will also hear an undying man.

Moreover, I never heard that ravens were made in the image of God; but I do find that as defiled, deformed, and debased as our race is, originally God said, *"Let us make man in our [own] image"* (Gen. 1:26). There is something about man that is not to be found in the lower creatures, the best and noblest of whom are immeasurably beneath the humblest child of Adam. There is a dignity about the fact of manhood that is not to be found in any of the beasts of the field. Behemoth and leviathan are put in subjection beneath the foot of man. The eagle cannot soar as high as man's soul mounts, nor the lion feed on such royal meat as man's spirit hungers after. Do you think that God will hear so low and so humble a creature as a raven and yet not hear you, when you are one of the race that was formed in His own image? Oh, do not think so harshly and so foolishly of Him whose ways are always just!

I will ask you this. Does not nature itself teach that man is to be cared for above the fowls of the air? If you heard the cries of young ravens, you might feel compassion enough for those birds to give them food if you knew how to feed them. But I cannot believe that any of you would help the birds and yet would not fly upon the wings of compassion to rescue a perishing infant, whose cries you might hear from the place where he was cast by cruel neglect. If, in the stillness of the night, you heard the plaintive cry of a man expiring in sickness, unpitied in the streets, would you not arise and help him? I am sure you would if you are one who would help a raven. If you have any compassion for a raven, much more would you have pity upon a man. Then, do you not think that God, the all-wise One, when He cares for these unfledged birds in the nest, would be sure also to care for you? Your heart says, "Yes." Henceforth, answer the unbelief of your heart by turning its own just reasoning against it.

But I hear you say, "Ah, but the raven is not sinful as I am. It may be an unclean bird, but it cannot be so unclean as I am morally. It may be black in hue, but I am black with sin. A raven cannot break the Sabbath, cannot swear, cannot commit adultery. A raven cannot be a drunkard. It cannot defile itself with vices such as those with which I am polluted."

I know all that, friend, and it may seem to you to make your case more hopeless, but I do not think it does so, really. Just think of it for a minute. What does this prove? Why, that you are a creature capable of sinning and, consequently, that you are an intelligent spirit living in a sense in which a raven does not live. You are a creature moving in the spirit world; you belong to the world of souls, in which the raven has no portion. The raven cannot sin because it has no spirit, no soul; but you are an intelligent agent, of which the better part is your soul.

Oh, if you will only think of it, you must see that it is not possible for a raven's cry to gain an audience of the ear of Divine Benevolence, and yet for your prayer to be despised and disregarded by the Most High.

> The insect that with puny wing,
> Just shoots along one summer's ray;
> The flow'ret, which the breath of Spring
> Wakes into life for half a day;
> The smallest mote, the tenderest hair,
> All feel our heavenly Father's care.

Surely, then, He will have respect to the cry of the humble, and He will not refuse their prayer.

I can hardly leave this point without remarking that the mention of a raven should encourage a sinner. As an old author has written,

> Among fowls He doth not mention the hawk or falcon, which are highly prized and fed by princes; nor the sweet singing nightingale, or such like musical pretty

birds, which men keep choicely and much delight in; but He chooses that hateful and malicious bird, the croaking raven, whom no man values but as she eats up the carrion, which might annoy him.

Behold, then, and wonder at the providence and kindness of God, that He should provide food for the raven, a creature of so dismal a hue and of so untuneable a tone, a creature that is so odious to most men, and ominous to some.

There is a great providence of God seen in providing for the ant, who gathers her meat in summer; but a greater in the raven, who, though he forgets, or is careless to provide for himself, yet God provides and layeth up for him. One would think the Lord should say of ravens, Let them shift for themselves or perish; no, the Lord God doth not despise any work of His hands; the raven hath his being from God, and therefore the raven shall be provided for by Him; not only the fair innocent dove, but the ugly raven hath his meat from God. Which clearly shows that the want of excellence in thee, thou black, raven-like sinner, will not prevent thy cry from being heard in heaven. Unworthiness the blood of Jesus shall remove, and defilement He shall utterly cleanse away. Only believe on Jesus, and thou shalt find peace.

A Better Cry

Then, in the next place, there is a great deal of difference between your cry and the cry of a raven. When the young ravens cry, I suppose they scarcely know what they want. They have a natural instinct that makes them cry for food, but their cry does not in itself express their want. You would soon find out, I suppose, that they meant food, but they have no articulate speech. They do not utter even a single word. It is just a constant, croaking, craving cry, and that is all.

But you know what you want, and few as your words are, your heart knows its own bitterness (Prov. 14:10) and dire distress. Your sighs and groans have an obvious meaning; your understanding is at the right hand of your needy heart. You know that you want peace and pardon; you know that you need Jesus, His precious blood, His perfect righteousness.

Now, if God hears such a strange, chattering, indistinct cry as that of a raven, do you not think that He will also hear the rational and expressive prayer of a poor, needy, guilty soul who is crying to Him, *"God be merciful to me a sinner"* (Luke 18:13)? Surely your reason tells you that!

Moreover, the young ravens cannot use arguments, for they have no understanding. They cannot say as you can,

> He knows what arguments I'd take
> To wrestle with my God,
> I'd plead for his own mercy's sake,
> And for a Savior's blood.

They have one argument, namely, their dire necessity, which forces their cry from them, but beyond this they cannot go; and even this they cannot set forth in order or describe in language. But you have a multitude of arguments ready at hand, and you have an understanding with which to set them in array and marshal them to besiege the throne of grace. Surely, if the mere plea of the unuttered want of the raven prevails with God, much more will you prevail with the Most High if you can argue your case before Him and come to Him with arguments in your mouth.

Come, you despairing one, and try my Lord! I do beseech you now to let that doleful ditty ascend into the ears of mercy! Open that bursting heart, and let it out in tears if words are beyond your power.

I fear, however, that a raven sometimes has a great advantage over some sinners who seek God in prayer, namely in this: young ravens are more in earnest about their food than some are about their souls. This, however, should not discourage you, but rather it should make you more earnest than you have been so far. When ravens want food, they do not cease crying until they have got it. There is no quieting a hungry, young raven until his mouth is full, and there is no quieting a sinner, when he is really in earnest, until he gets his heart full of divine mercy.

I desire that some of you would pray more vehemently! *"The kingdom of heaven suffereth violence, and the violent take it by force"* (Matt. 11:12). An old Puritan said, "Prayer is a cannon set at the gate of heaven to burst open its gates." You must take the city by storm if you would have it. You will not ride to heaven on a featherbed; you must go on a pilgrimage. There is no going to the land of glory while you are sound asleep; dreamy sluggards will have to wake up in hell. If God has made you feel in your soul the need of salvation, cry like one who is awake and alive. Be in earnest; cry aloud; spare not. Then I think you will find that if He hears such a cry as the raven's, it is much more certain that He will hear yours.

A More Noble Request

Remember that the matter of your prayer is more congenial to the ear of God than the raven's cry for meat. All that the young ravens cry for is food; give them a little carrion, and they are done. Your cry must be much more pleasing to God's ear, for you entreat for forgiveness through the blood of His dear Son. It is a nobler occupation for the Most High to bestow spiritual rather than natural gifts. The streams of grace flow from the upper springs. I know He is so gracious that He does not dishonor Himself even when He drops food into the young raven's mouth; but still, there is more dignity about the work of giving peace and pardon and reconciliation to the sons of men. Eternal love appointed a way of mercy from before the foundation of the world, and infinite wisdom is engaged with boundless power to carry out the divine design. Surely the Lord must take much pleasure in saving the sons of men.

If God is pleased to supply the beasts of the field, do you not think that He delights much more to supply His own children? I think you would find more congenial employment in teaching your own children than you would in merely foddering your oxen or scattering barley among the fowls at the barn door, because there would be in the first work something nobler, which would more fully call up all your powers and bring out your inward self. I am not left here to conjecture. It is written, *"He delighteth in mercy"* (Mic. 7:18). When God uses His power, He cannot be sad, for He is a happy God. But if there is such a thing possible as the Infinite Deity being more happy at one time than at another, it is when He is forgiving sinners through the precious blood of Jesus.

Ah, sinner, when you cry to God, you give Him an opportunity to do that which He loves most to do; for He delights to forgive, to press His Ephraim to His bosom, to say of His prodigal son, *"This my son was dead, and is alive again; he was lost, and is found"* (Luke 15:24). This is more comfortable to the Father's heart than feeding the fatted calf or tending the cattle of a thousand hills.

Since, dear friends, you are asking for something that will honor God far more to give than the mere gift of food to ravens, I think there comes a very forcible blow of my argumentative hammer to break your unbelief in pieces. May God the Holy Spirit, the true Comforter, work in you mightily! Surely the God who gives food to ravens will not deny peace and pardon to seeking sinners. Try Him! Try

Him at this moment! No, do not run away! Try Him now.

A Divine Warrant

We must not pause on any one point when the whole subject is so prolific. There is another source of comfort for you, namely, that the ravens are nowhere commanded to cry. When they cry, their petition is unwarranted by any specific exhortation from the divine mouth, while you have a warrant derived from divine exhortations to approach the throne of God in prayer. If a rich man would open his house to those who were not invited, he would surely receive those who were invited. Ravens come without being invited, yet they are not sent away empty. You come as an invited guest; how can you be denied?

Do you think you are not invited? Listen to this: *"Whoever shall call on the name of the Lord shall be saved"* (Acts 2:21). *"Call upon me in the day of trouble: I will deliver thee, and thou shalt glorify me"* (Ps. 50:15). *"Go ye into all the world, and preach the gospel to every creature. He that believeth and is baptized shall be saved; but he that believeth not shall be damned"* (Mark 16:15–16). *"Believe on the Lord Jesus Christ, and thou shalt be saved"*

(Acts 16:31). *"Repent, and be baptized every one of you in the name of Jesus Christ for the remission of sins"* (Acts 2:38).

These are exhortations given without any limitation as to character. They freely invite you; no, they beseech you to come. Oh, after this can you think that God will spurn you? The window is open, the raven flies in, and the God of mercy does not chase it out. The door is open, and the word of promise invites you to come; do not think that He will give you a denial. Rather, believe that He will receive you graciously and love you freely, and then you will *"render* [to him] *the calves of* [your] *lips"* (Hos. 14:2). At any rate, try Him! Try Him even now!

A Work of Grace

Again, there is yet another, far mightier argument. The cry of a young raven is nothing but the natural cry of a creature, but your cry, if it is sincere, is the result of a work of grace in your heart. When the raven cries to heaven, it is nothing but the raven's own self that cries. But when you cry, *"God be merciful to me a sinner"* (Luke 18:13), it is God the Holy Spirit crying in you. It is the new life that God has given you crying to the Source from where it came to have further communion and communication in sincerity and in truth.

We can, if we think it right, teach our children to "say their prayers," but we cannot teach them to pray. You may make a prayer book, but you cannot put a grain of prayer into a book, for it is too spiritual a matter to be put on pages. Some of you, perhaps, may read prayers in the family. I will not denounce the practice, but I will say this much about it: you may read those prayers for seventy years, and yet you may never once pray, for prayer is quite a different thing from mere words.

True prayer is the trading of the heart with God, and the heart never comes into spiritual commerce with the ports of heaven until God the Holy Spirit puts wind into the sails and speeds the ship into its haven. *"Ye must be born again"* (John 3:7). If there is any real prayer in your heart, though you may not know the secret, God the Holy Spirit is there.

Now, if He hears cries that do not come from Himself, how much more will He hear those that do! Perhaps you have been puzzling yourself to know whether your cry is a natural or a spiritual one. This may seem very important, and doubtless it is; but whether your cry is either the one or the other, still continue to seek the Lord. Possibly, you doubt whether natural cries are heard by God; let me assure you that they are.

I remember saying something on this subject on one occasion in a certain ultra-Calvinistic place of worship. At that time I was preaching to children, and I was exhorting them to pray. I happened to say that, long before any actual conversion, I had prayed for common mercies and that God had heard my prayers.

This did not suit my good friends of that superfine school. Afterwards they all came around me professedly to know what I meant but really to quibble and nag according to their nature and habit. *"They compassed me about like bees"* (Ps. 118:12); yes, like bees they compassed me about! To say that God hears the prayer of natural men was something worse than Arminianism, if indeed anything could be worse to them. "How could it be that God could hear a natural prayer?" And while I paused for a moment, an old woman in a red cloak pushed her way into the little circle around me and said to them in a very forcible way, like a mother in Israel as she was, "Why do you raise this question, forgetting what God Himself has said? What is this you say, that God does not hear natural prayer? Why, does He not hear the young ravens when they cry unto Him, and do you think they offer spiritual prayers?" Immediately, the men of war took to their heels; no defeat was more thorough. For once in their lives they must have felt that they might possibly err.

Surely, friends, this may encourage and comfort you. I am not going to give you just now the task of finding out whether your prayers are natural or spiritual, whether they come from God's Spirit or whether they do not, because that might, perhaps, nonplus you. If the prayer proceeds from your very heart, we know how it got there, though you may not. God hears the ravens, and I do believe He will hear you. I will tell you something else I believe about prayer, though I do not want it to raise questions in your heart now. God hears your prayer because—though you may not know it—there is a secret work of the Spirit of God going on within you that is teaching you to pray.

A Mighty Prayer Partner

But I have mightier arguments, and nearer the mark. When the young ravens cry, they cry alone; but when you pray, you have a mightier One than you praying with you. Hear that sinner crying, *"God be merciful to me a sinner"* (Luke 18:13). Listen! Do you hear that other cry that goes up with his? No, you do not hear it because your ears are dull and heavy, but God hears it. There is another voice, far louder and sweeter than the first and far more powerful, mounting up at the same moment and pleading, "Father, forgive them through My precious blood." The echo to the sinner's whisper is as majestic as the thunder's peal. Never does a sinner truly pray without Christ praying at the same time. You cannot see or hear Him, but never does Jesus stir the depths of your soul by His Spirit without His soul being stirred, too. Oh, sinner! Your prayer, when it comes before God, is a very different thing from what it is when it issues forth from you.

Sometimes poor people come to us with petitions that they wish to send to some company or important person. They bring the petition and ask us to have it presented for them. It is very badly spelled, very strangely written, and we can barely make out what they mean; but still there is enough to let us know what they want. First of all, we make out a good copy for them, and then, having stated their case, we put our own name at the bottom. If we have any influence, of course they get what they desire through the power of the name signed at the foot of the petition.

This is just what the Lord Jesus Christ does with our poor prayers. He makes a good copy of them, stamps them with the seal of His own atoning blood, puts His own name at the foot, and thus they go up to God's throne. It is your prayer, but, oh, it is His prayer, too. It is the fact of its being His prayer that makes it prevail.

Now, this is a sledgehammer argument: If the ravens prevail when they cry all alone, if just their poor chattering brings them what they want, how much more will the plaintive petitions of the poor, trembling sinner prevail. For the sinner can say, "For Jesus' sake" and can clench all his own arguments with the blessed plea, "The Lord Jesus Christ deserves it; O Lord, give it to me for His sake."

I have been writing this to seeking ones, who have been crying so long and yet are afraid that they will never be heard. I do trust that they may not have to wait much longer but may soon have a gracious answer of peace. And if they do not get the desires of their hearts just yet, I hope that they may be encouraged to persevere until the day of grace dawns. You have a promise that the ravens have not, and that might make another argument, if space permitted us to dwell upon it. Trembler, having a promise to plead, never fear, but speed to the throne of grace!

Encouragement for Sinners

And now, let me say to the sinner, in closing, that if you have cried unsuccessfully, still cry on. *"Go again seven times"* (1 Kings 18:43), yes, and seventy times seven. Remember that the mercy of God in Christ Jesus is your only hope; cling to it, then, as a drowning man clings to the only rope within reach. If you perish praying for mercy through the precious blood, you will be the first that ever perished that way. Cry on; just cry on. But, believe, too, for believing brings the morning star and the day dawn.

When John Ryland's wife Betty lay dying, she was in great distress of mind, though she had been a Christian for many years. Her husband said to her in his quaint but wise way, "Well, Betty, what ails you?"

"Oh, John, I am dying, and I have no hope, John!"

"But, my dear, where are you going then?"

"I am going to hell!" was the answer.

"Well," said he, covering up his deep anguish with his usual humor and meaning to strike a blow that would be sure to hit the nail on the head and put her doubts to speedy flight, "what do you intend to do when you get there, Betty?" The good woman could give no answer, and Mr. Ryland continued, "Do you think you will pray when you get there?"

"Oh, John," she said, "I would pray anywhere; I cannot help praying!"

"Well, then," said he, "they will say, 'Here is Betty Ryland praying here; throw her out. We won't have anybody praying here; throw her out!'"

This strange way of putting it brought light to her soul. She saw at once the absurdity of the idea of a soul really seeking Christ and yet being cast away forever from His presence.

Cry on, soul; cry on! While the child can cry, it lives; and while you can besiege the throne of mercy, there is hope for you. But hear as well as cry, and believe what you hear, for it is by believing that peace is obtained.

What is it you are looking for? Some of you are expecting to see bright visions, but I hope you may never be gratified, for they are not worth a penny a thousand. All the visions in the world since the days of miracles, put together, are but mere dreams after all, and dreams are nothing but vanity. People eat too much supper and then dream; it is indigestion or a morbid activity of the brain, and that is all. If that is all the evidence you have of conversion, you will do well to doubt it. I pray you will never rest satisfied with it; it is wretched rubbish to build your eternal hopes upon.

Perhaps you are looking for very strange feelings—not quite an electric shock, but something very singular and peculiar. Believe me, you need never feel the strange motions that you prize so highly. All those strange feelings that some people speak of in connection with conversion may or may not be of any good to them, but I am certain that they really have nothing to do with conversion so as to be at all necessary to it.

I will put a question or two to you. Do you believe yourself to be a sinner? "Yes," you say. But, supposing I put that word *sinner* away, do you mean that you believe you have broken God's law, that you are a good-for-nothing offender against God's government? Do you believe that you have in your heart, at any rate, broken all the commandments and that you deserve punishment accordingly? "Yes," you say, "I not only believe that, but I feel it; it is a burden that I carry around with me daily." Now, something more, do you believe that the Lord Jesus Christ can put all this sin of yours away? "Yes, I do believe that." Then, can you trust Him to save you? You want saving; you cannot save yourself; can you trust Him to save you? "Yes," you say, "I already do that." Well, my dear friend, if you really trust Jesus, it is certain that you are saved, for you have the only evidence of salvation that is continual with any of us. There are other evidences that follow afterwards, such as holiness and the graces of the Spirit, but the only evidence that is continual with the best of men living is this:

> Nothing in my hands I bring,
>   Simply to thy cross I cling.

Can you use Jack the huckster's verse?

> I'm a poor sinner and nothing at all,
>   But Jesus Christ is my all-in-all.

I hope you will go a great deal further in experience on some points than this by and by, but I do not want you to advance an inch further as to the ground of your evidence and the reason for your hope. Just stop there. If now you look away from everything that is within you or without you to Jesus Christ, if now you trust His sufferings on Calvary and His whole atoning work as the ground of your acceptance before God, you are saved. You do not need anything more; you have *"passed from death unto life"* (John 5:24). *"He that believeth on him is not condemned"* (John 3:18). *"He that believeth on the Son hath everlasting life"* (John 3:36).

If I were to meet an angel in the aisle of the church and he should say, "Charles Spurgeon, I have come from heaven to tell you that you are pardoned," I would say to him, "I know that I am pardoned without your telling me so; I know it on a much greater authority than yours." If he asked me how I knew it, I would reply, "The word of God is better to me than the word of any angel, and God has said it: *'He that believeth on him is not condemned'* (John 3:18). I do believe on Him, and therefore I am not condemned, and I know it without an angel telling me so."

You troubled ones, do not look for angels and tokens and evidences and signs. If you rest on the finished work of Jesus, you already have the best evidence of your salvation in the world. You have God's word for it; what more is needed? Cannot you accept God's word? You can accept your father's word; you can accept your mother's word; why can you not accept God's word? Oh, what bad hearts we must have to distrust God Himself! Perhaps you say you would not do such a thing. Oh, but you do doubt God if you do not trust Christ, for *"he that believeth not God hath made him a liar"* (1 John 5:10). If you do not trust Christ, you do in effect say that God is a liar. You do not want to say that, do you?

Oh, believe the truthfulness of God! May the Spirit of God constrain you to believe the Father's mercy, the power of the Son's blood, the willingness of the Holy Spirit to bring sinners to Himself! Come, my dear friends, join with me in prayer that you may be led by grace to see in Jesus all that you need.

Prayer is a creature's strength, his very breath
    and being;
Prayer is the golden key that can open the wicket
    of mercy;
Prayer is the magic sound that saith to fate, so
    be it;
Prayer is the slender nerve that moveth the
    muscles of Omnipotence.
Wherefore, pray, O creature, for many and great
    are thy wants;
Thy mind, thy conscience, and thy being, thy
    needs commend thee unto prayer,
The cure of all cares, the grand panacea for all
    pains,
Doubt's destroyer, ruin's remedy, the antidote to
    all anxieties.

Chapter Three

Order and Argument
in Prayer

Oh that I knew where I might find him!
that I might come even to his seat! I would
order my cause before him, and fill my
mouth with arguments.
—Job 23:3–4

In Job's uttermost extremity he cried after the Lord. The longing desire of an afflicted child of God is to see his Father's face once more. His first prayer is not, "Oh, that I might be healed of the disease which now festers in every part of my body!" Nor is it even, "Oh, that I might see my children restored from the jaws of the grave and my property once more brought from the hand of the spoiler!" But the first and uppermost cry is, "Oh, that I knew where to find Him who is my God! Oh, that I might come even to His seat!" God's children run home when the storm comes on.

It is the heaven-born instinct of a gracious soul to seek shelter from all problems beneath the wings of Jehovah. "He who has made God his refuge" might serve as the title of a true believer. A hypocrite, when he feels that he has been afflicted by God, resents the infliction and, like a slave, would run from the Master who has scourged him. The true heir of heaven does not do so. He kisses the hand that struck him, and he seeks shelter from the rod in the bosom of that very God who frowned upon him.

You will observe that the desire to commune with God is intensified by the failure of all other sources of consolation. When Job first saw his friends at a distance, he may have entertained a hope that their kind counsel and compassionate tenderness would blunt the edge of his grief. However, they had not spoken long before he cried out in bitterness, *"Miserable comforters are ye all"* (Job 16:2). They put salt into his wounds, they heaped fuel upon the flame of his sorrow, and they added the gall of their reproaches to the wormwood of his griefs. In the sunshine of his smile they once had longed to sun themselves, and now they dare to cast shadows upon his reputation, most ungenerous and undeserved.

Alas for the poor man when his wine cup mocks him with vinegar and his pillow pricks him with thorns! The patriarch turned away from his sorry friends and looked up to the celestial throne, just as a traveler turns from his empty skin bottle and runs full speed to the well. He bids farewell to earthborn hopes and cries, *"Oh that I knew where I might find* [my God]!"

My friends, nothing teaches us so much the preciousness of the Creator as when we learn the emptiness of all besides. When you have been pierced through and through with the sentence, *"Cursed be the man that trusteth in man, and maketh flesh his arm"* (Jer. 17:5), then you will suck unutterable sweetness from the divine assurance, *"Blessed is the man that trusteth in the LORD, and whose hope the LORD is"* (Jer. 17:7). Turning away with bitter scorn from earth's hives, where you found no honey but many sharp stings, you will rejoice in Him whose faithful word is sweeter than honey or the honeycomb.

It is further observable that although a good man hastens to God in his trouble, although he runs with all the more speed because of the unkindness of his fellowmen, sometimes the gracious soul is left without the comfortable presence of God. This is the worst of all griefs. The text of this chapter is one of Job's deep groans, far deeper than any that came from him on account of the loss of his children and his property: *"Oh that I knew where I might find him!"* The worst of all losses is to lose the smile of God. He now had a foretaste of the bitterness of his Redeemer's cry, *"My God, my God, why hast thou forsaken me?"* (Matt. 27:46). God's presence is always with His people in one sense, as far as secretly sustaining them is concerned, but His manifest presence they do not always enjoy. You may be beloved of God and yet have no consciousness of that love in your soul. You may be as dear to His heart as Jesus Christ Himself; yet for a small moment He may forsake you, and in a little wrath He may hide Himself from you (Isa. 54:7–8).

But, dear friends, at such times the desire of the believing soul gathers yet greater intensity from the fact of God's light being withheld. The gracious soul addresses itself with a double zeal to find God, and it sends up its groans, its entreaties, its sobs, and its sighs to heaven more frequently and fervently. *"Oh that I knew where I might find him!"* Distance or labor are as nothing; if the soul only knew where to go, it would soon overleap the distance. That seems to me to be the state of mind in which Job pronounced the words of our text.

We cannot stop on this point, for the object of this chapter beckons us onward. It appears that Job's end in desiring the presence of God was that he might pray to Him. He had prayed, but he wanted to pray as in God's presence. He desired to plead as before one whom he knew would hear and help him. He longed to state his own case before the seat of the impartial Judge, before the very face of the all-wise God. He would appeal from the lower courts, where his friends judged unrighteous judgment, to the Court of King's Bench—the high court of heaven. "There," he says, *"I would order my cause before him, and fill my mouth with arguments."*

In this verse Job teaches us how he meant to plead and intercede with God. He does, as it were, reveal the secrets of his closet and unveil the art of prayer. We are here admitted into the guild of suppliants; we are shown the art and mystery of pleading; we have here taught to us the blessed handicraft and science of prayer. If we can be bound apprentice to Job for the next chapter and can have a lesson from Job's Master, we may acquire great skill in interceding with God.

There are two things here set forth as necessary in prayer: ordering our cause and filling our mouths with arguments. We will speak of those two things, and then if we have rightly learned the lesson, a blessed result will follow.

Ordering Our Cause

First, it is needful that our suit be ordered before God. There is a vulgar notion that prayer is a very easy thing, a kind of common business that may be done in any way, without care or effort. Some think that you just have to get a book from the shelf and get through a certain number of very excellent words and you have prayed and may put the book back. Others suppose that to use a book is superstitious and that you ought rather to repeat extemporaneous sentences, sentences that come to your mind with a rush, like a herd of swine or a pack of hounds. They think that when you have uttered them with a little attention to what you have said, you have prayed.

Now, neither of these modes of prayer were adopted by ancient saints. They appear to have thought a great deal more seriously about prayer than many do nowadays. The ancient saints were accustomed, with Job, to ordering their cause before God. For example, a petitioner coming into court does not come there to state his case on the spur of the moment. Certainly not. He enters into the audience chamber with his suit well prepared. Moreover, he has learned how he ought to behave himself in the presence of the great one to whom he is appealing. In times of peril and distress we may fly to God just as we are, as the dove enters the cleft of the rock even though her plumes are ruffled; however, in ordinary times we should not come with an unprepared spirit, even as a child does not come to his father in the morning until he has washed his face.

See yonder priest. He has a sacrifice to offer, but he does not rush into the court of the priests and hack at the bull with the first ax he can find. He first washes his feet at the brazen basin; he puts on his garments and adorns himself with his priestly clothing. Then he comes to the altar with his victim properly divided according to the law. He is careful to do according to the command. He takes the blood in a bowl and pours it in an appropriate place at the foot of the altar, not throwing it just as it may occur to him; and he kindles the fire with the sacred fire from off of the altar, not with common flame.

Now this ritual is all set aside, but the truth that it taught remains the same: our spiritual sacrifices should be offered with holy carefulness. God forbid that our prayer should be a mere leaping out of one's bed and kneeling down and saying anything that comes first to mind; on the contrary, may we wait upon the Lord with holy fear and sacred awe.

See how David prayed when God had blessed him. He went in before the Lord—understand that. He did not stand outside at a distance, but he went in before the Lord and sat down. (Sitting is not a bad posture for prayer, even if some do speak against it.) Sitting down quietly and calmly before the Lord, he then began to pray, but not until he had first thought over the divine goodness and so attained to the spirit of prayer. By the assistance of the Holy Spirit, he opened his mouth. Oh, that we more often sought the Lord is this style!

Abraham may serve as an example. He rose up early—here was his willingness. He went three days' journey—here was his zeal. He left his servants at the foot of the hill—here was his privacy. He carried the wood and the fire with him—here was his preparation. Lastly, he built the altar and laid the wood in order and then took the knife—here was the devout carefulness of his worship.

David put it this way: *"In the morning will I direct my prayer unto thee, and will look up"* (Ps. 5:3). This Scripture means that he marshaled his thoughts like men of war or that he aimed his prayers like arrows. He did not take the arrow and put it on the bowstring and just shoot anywhere. After he had taken out the chosen shaft and fitted it to the string, he took deliberate aim. He looked—looked well— at the center of the target. He kept his eye fixed on it, directing his prayer, and then drew his bow with all his strength and let the arrow fly. Then, when the shaft had left his hand, what does he say? "[I] *will look up.*" He looked up to see where the arrow went, to see what effect it had, for he expected an answer to his prayers; he was not like many who scarcely think of their prayers after they have uttered them. David knew that he had an engagement before him that required all his mental powers. He marshaled his faculties and went about the work in a workmanlike manner, as one who believed in it and meant to succeed.

We should plow carefully and pray carefully. The better the work, the more attention it deserves. To be anxious in the shop and thoughtless in the prayer closet is little less than blasphemy, for it is an insinuation that anything will do for God but the world must have our best.

If any ask what order should be observed in prayer, I am not about to give you a scheme such as many have drawn up, in which adoration, confession, petition, intercession, and ascription are arranged in succession. I am not persuaded that any such order is of divine authority. It is no mere mechanical order I have been referring to, for our prayers will be equally acceptable, and possibly equally proper, in any form. There are specimens of prayers in all shapes in the Old and New Testaments.

The true spiritual order of prayer seems to me to consist of something more than mere arrangement. It is most fitting for us first to feel that we are now doing something that is real. We are about to address ourselves to God, whom we cannot see but who is really present. We can neither touch nor hear nor by our senses comprehend Him, but, nevertheless, He is as truly with us as though we were speaking to a friend of flesh and blood like ourselves. Feeling the reality of God's presence, our mind will be led by divine grace into a humble state. We will feel like Abraham when he said, *"I have taken upon me to speak unto the Lord, which am but dust and ashes"* (Gen. 18:27). Consequently, we will not deliver ourselves of our prayer as boys repeating their lessons, as a mere matter of rote. Much less will we speak as if we were rabbis instructing our pupils or, as I have heard some do, with the coarseness of a robber stopping a person on the road and demanding his money. No, we will be humble yet bold petitioners, humbly asking mercy through the Savior's blood.

When I feel that I am in the presence of God and I take my rightful position in His presence, the next thing I will want to recognize will be that I have no right to what I am seeking and cannot expect to obtain it except as a gift of grace. I must recollect that God limits the channel through which He will give me mercy: He will give it to me through His dear Son. Let me put myself then under the patronage of the Great Redeemer. Let me feel that now it is no longer I who speak but Christ who speaks with me. While I plead, I plead His wounds, His life, His death, His blood, Himself. This is truly getting into order.

The next thing is to consider what I am going to ask for. It is most proper in prayer to aim at great distinctness of supplication. It is good not to beat around the bush in prayer, but to come directly to the point. I like that prayer of Abraham's, *"O that Ishmael might live before thee!"* (Gen. 17:18). There is the name of the person prayed for and the blessing desired, all put in a few words: *"that Ishmael might live before thee."* Many people would have used a roundabout expression of this kind: "Oh, that our beloved offspring might be regarded with the favor that You so graciously bear to those who..." Say "Ishmael" if you mean Ishmael. Put it in plain words before the Lord.

Some people cannot even pray for the minister without using such indirect descriptions that one might think it were the church usher or somebody that should not be mentioned too particularly. Why not be distinct and say what we mean as well as mean what we say? Ordering our cause would bring us to greater distinctness of mind.

It is not necessary, my dear friends, in the prayer closet to ask for every supposable good thing. It is not necessary to rehearse the catalog of every want that you may have, have had, can have, or will have. Ask for what you need now, and, as a rule, keep to present need. Ask for your daily bread—what you want now—ask for that. Ask for it plainly, as before God, who does not regard your fine expressions. To Him your eloquence and oratory will be less than nothing and vanity. You are before the Lord; let your words be few, but let your heart be fervent.

You have not quite completed the ordering when you have asked for what you want through Jesus Christ. You should look at the blessing that you desire, to see whether it is assuredly a fitting thing to ask. Some prayers would never be offered if people would only think. A little reflection would show us that some things that we desire were better left alone. We may, moreover, have a motive at the bottom of our desire that is not Christ-like, a selfish motive that forgets God's glory and caters only to our own ease and comfort. Now, although we may ask for things that are for our profit, still we must never let our profit interfere in any way with the glory of God. There must be mingled with acceptable prayer the holy salt of submission to the divine will.

I like Luther's saying: "Lord, I *will* have my will of Thee at this time." "What!" you gasp. "You like such an expression as that?" I do, because of the next clause, which was, "I will have my will, for I know that my will is Thy will." That is well spoken, Luther, but without the last words it would have been wicked presumption.

When we are sure that what we ask for is for God's glory, then, if we have power in prayer, we may say, *"I will not let thee go, except thou bless me"* (Gen. 32:26). We may come to close dealings with God, and, like

Jacob with the angel, we may even put it to the wrestle and seek to give the angel the fall sooner than be sent away without the blessing. However, we must be quite clear before we come to those terms that what we are seeking is really for the Master's honor.

Put these three things together: deep spirituality, which recognizes prayer as being real conversation with the invisible God; much distinctness, which is the reality of prayer, asking for what we want with much fervency, believing the thing to be necessary and therefore resolving to obtain it if it can be had by prayer; and above all these, complete submission, leaving it still with the Master's will. Commingle all these, and you have a clear idea of what it means to order your cause before the Lord.

Still, prayer itself is an art that only the Holy Spirit can teach us. He is the giver of all prayer. Pray for prayer. Pray until you can pray. Pray to be helped to pray, and do not give up praying because you cannot pray. It is when you think you cannot pray that you are most praying. Sometimes, when you have no sort of comfort in your supplications, it is then that your heart, all broken and cast down, is really wrestling and truly prevailing with the Most High.

Filling the Mouth with Arguments

The second part of prayer is filling the mouth with arguments. Not filling the mouth with words or good phrases or pretty expressions, but filling the mouth with arguments. The ancient saints were known to argue in prayer. When we come to the gate of mercy, forcible arguments are the knocks of the rapper by which the gate is opened.

"Why are arguments to be used at all?" one may inquire. The reply is, Certainly not because God is slow to give, not because we can change the divine purpose, not because God needs to be informed of any circumstance with regard to ourselves or of anything in connection with the mercy asked; the arguments to be used are for our own benefit, not for His. He requires us to plead with Him and to *"bring forth* [our] *strong reasons"* (Isa. 41:21) because this will show that we feel the value of the mercy. When a man searches for arguments for a thing, it is because he attaches importance to that which he is seeking.

The best prayers I have ever heard in our prayer meetings have been those which have been most full of argument. Sometimes my soul has been melted down, so to speak, when I have listened to friends who have come before

75

God feeling that the mercy is really needed and that they must have it. They first pleaded with God to give it for this reason, then for a second, then for a third, and then for a fourth and a fifth, until they have awakened the fervency of the entire assembly.

My friends, there is no need for prayer at all as far as God is concerned, but what a need there is for it on our own account! If we were not constrained to pray, I question whether we could even live as Christians. If God's mercies came to us unasked, they would not be half as useful as they now are, when they have to be sought for. Now we get a double blessing, a blessing in the obtaining and a blessing in the seeking.

The very act of prayer is a blessing. To pray is, as it were, to bathe in a cool, swirling stream and so to escape from the heat of earth's summer sun. To pray is to mount on eagle's wings above the clouds and get into the clear heaven where God dwells. To pray is to enter the treasure-house of God and to gather riches out of an inexhaustible storehouse. To pray is to grasp heaven in one's arms, to embrace the Deity within one's soul, and to feel one's body made a temple of the Holy Spirit.

Apart from the answer, prayer in itself is a blessing. To pray, my friends, is to cast off your burdens. It is to tear away your rags; it is to shake off your diseases; it is to be filled with spiritual vigor; it is to reach the highest point of Christian health. God grant us to be much in the holy art of arguing with God in prayer.

A Catalog of Arguments

The most interesting part of our subject remains. It is a very rapid summary and catalog of a few of the arguments that have been used with great success with God.

God's Attributes

It is well in prayer to plead with Jehovah His attributes. Abraham did so when he laid hold upon God's justice. Sodom was to be pleaded for, and Abraham begins,

> *Peradventure there be fifty righteous within the city: wilt thou also destroy and not spare the place for the fifty righteous that are therein? That be far from thee to do after this manner, to slay the righteous with the wicked: and that the righteous should be as the wicked, that be far from thee: Shall not the Judge of all the earth do right?*
> (Gen. 18:24–25)

77

Here the wrestling begins. It was a powerful argument by which the patriarch grasped the Lord's left hand and arrested it just when the thunderbolt was about to fall. But there came a reply to it. It was hinted to him that this would not spare the city. Then you notice how the good man, when sorely pressed, retreated by inches. At last, when he could no longer lay hold upon justice, he grasped God's right hand of mercy—that gave him a wondrous hold—when he asked that the city might be spared if there were only ten righteous.

So you and I may take hold at any time upon the justice, the mercy, the faithfulness, the wisdom, the long-suffering, the tenderness of God; and we will find every attribute of the Most High to be, as it were, a great battering ram with which we may open the gates of heaven.

God's Promise

Another mighty piece of ordinance in the battle of prayer is God's promise. When Jacob was on the other side of the brook Jabbok and his brother Esau was coming with armed men, he pleaded with God not to allow Esau to destroy the mother and the children. As a master reason he pleaded, *"And thou saidst, I will surely do thee good"* (Gen. 32:12). Oh, the force of that plea! He was holding God to His word: *"Thou saidst."* The attribute is a splendid horn of the altar to lay hold upon; but the promise, which has in it the attribute and something more, is a yet mightier hold-fast. *"Thou saidst."*

Remember how David put it. After Nathan had spoken the promise, David said at the close of his prayer, *"Do as thou hast said"* (2 Sam. 7:25). *"Do as thou hast said."* That is a legitimate argument with every honest man. *"God is not a man, that he should lie...hath he said, and shall he not do it? or hath he spoken, and shall he not make it good?"* (Num. 23:19). *"Let God be true, but every man a liar"* (Rom. 3:4). Will He not be true? Will He not keep His word? Will not every word that comes out of His lips stand fast and be fulfilled?

Solomon, at the opening of the temple, used this same mighty plea. He pleads with God to remember the word that He had spoken to his father David and to bless that place.

When a man gives a promissory note, his honor is engaged. He signs it with his signature, and he must discharge it when the due time comes, or else he loses credit. It will never be said that God dishonors His bills. The credit of the Most High never was impeached and never will be. He is punctual to the moment; He is never before His time, but He is never behind it. You can search this Book through and compare it with the experience of God's people, and the two match from the first to the last. Many an agèd patriarch has said with Joshua in his old age, *"There failed not ought of any good thing which the LORD had spoken...all came to pass"* (Josh. 21:45).

My friend, if you have a divine promise, you need not plead it with an "if" in it; you may plead with a certainty. If, for the mercy that you are now asking, you have God's solemnly pledged word, there will scarcely be any room for caution about submission to His will. You know His will. That will is in the promise. Plead it. Do not give Him rest until He fulfills it. He meant to fulfill it, or else He would not have given it.

The Great Name of God

A third argument to be used is that employed by Moses: the great name of God. How mightily did he argue with God on one occasion upon this ground! "What will You do for Your great name? The Egyptians will say, 'Because the Lord could not bring them into the land, therefore He slew them in the wilderness.'" (See Exodus 32:12; Numbers 14:13–16.)

There are some occasions when the name of God is very closely tied up with the history of His people. Sometimes in reliance upon a divine promise, a believer will be led to take a certain course of action. Now, if the Lord should not be as good as His promise, not only is the believer deceived, but the wicked world looking on would say, "Aha! Aha! Where is your God?"

Take the case of our respected brother, Mr. Müller, of Bristol. These many years he has declared that God hears prayer, and firm in that conviction, he has gone on to build house after house for the maintenance of orphans. Now, I can very well conceive that, if he were driven to a point of need for the maintenance of those one or two thousand children, he might very well use the plea, "What will You do for Your great name?"

And you, in some severe trouble, when you have received the promise, may say, "Lord, You have said, 'In six troubles I will be with you, and in seven I will not forsake you.' (See Job 5:19.) I have told my friends and neighbors that I put my trust in You, and if You do not deliver me now, where is Your name? Arise, O

God, and do this thing, lest Your honor be cast into the dust."

The Sorrows of His People

We may also plead the sorrows of His people. This is frequently done. Jeremiah is the great master of this art. He says,

> *Her Nazarites were purer than snow, they were whiter than milk, they were more ruddy in body than rubies, their polishing was of sapphire: Their visage is blacker than a coal.* (Lam. 4:7–8)

> *The precious sons of Zion, comparable to fine gold, how are they esteemed as earthen pitchers, the work of the hands of the potter!* (Lam. 4:2)

He talks of all their griefs and distresses in the siege. He calls upon the Lord to look upon His suffering Zion, and before long his plaintive cries are heard.

Nothing is so eloquent with a father as his child's cry. Yes, there is one thing more mighty still, and that is a moan—when the child is so sick that he is past crying and lies moaning with the kind of moan that indicates extreme suffering and intense weakness. Who can resist that moan? Ah, and when God's Israel will be brought very low so that they can scarcely cry but only their moans are heard, then comes the Lord's time of deliverance, and He is sure to show that He loves His people.

Dear friends, whenever you also are brought into the same condition, you may plead your moanings; and when you see a church brought very low, you may use her griefs as an argument as to why God should return and save the remnant of His people.

The Past

Friends, it is good to plead the past with God. Ah, you experienced people of God, you know how to do this. Here is David's specimen of it: *"Thou hast been my help; leave me not, neither forsake me"* (Ps. 27:9). He pleads God's mercy to him from his youth up. He speaks of being cast upon his God from his very birth, and then he pleads, *"Now also when I am old and greyheaded, O God, forsake me not"* (Ps. 71:18). Moses also, speaking with God, says, "You brought this people up out of Egypt." (See Numbers 14:13.) As if he would say, "Do not leave Your work unfinished. You have begun to build; complete it. You have fought the first battle; Lord, end the campaign! Go on until You get a complete victory."

How often have we cried in our trouble, "Lord, You delivered me in such and such a sharp trial, when it seemed as if no help were near; You have never forsaken me yet. I have set up my Ebenezer in Your name. If You had intended to leave me, why have You showed me such things? Have You brought Your servant to this place to put him to shame?"

Friends, we deal with an unchanging God, who will do in the future what He has done in the past because He never turns from His purpose and cannot be thwarted in His design. The past thus becomes a very mighty means of winning blessings from Him.

The Only True God

There was once an occasion when the very existence and true deity of Jehovah became a triumphant plea for the prophet Elijah. On that august occasion, when he had bidden his adversaries to see whether their god could answer them by fire, you can little guess the excitement there must have been that day in the prophet's mind. With what stern sarcasm did he say, *"Cry aloud: for he is a god; either he is talking, or he is pursuing, or he is in a journey,*

*or peradventure he sleepeth, and must be awak-
ened"* (1 Kings 18:27). And as they cut themselves with knives and leaped upon the altar,
oh, the scorn with which that man of God must
have looked down upon their impotent exer-
tions and their earnest but useless cries!

But think of how his heart might have
palpitated if it had not been for the strength of
his faith, when he repaired the altar of God
that was broken down, laid the wood in order,
and killed the bull. Hear him cry, "Pour water
on it. You will not suspect me of concealing
fire. Pour water on the victim." When they had
done so, he bids them, "Do it a second time,"
and they did it a second time. Then he says,
"Do it a third time." And when it was all cov-
ered with water, soaked and saturated
through, then he stands up and cries to God,
*"Let it be known this day that thou art God in
Israel"* (1 Kings 18:36).

Here everything was put to the test. Jehovah's own existence was now put, as it were, at
stake before the eyes of men by this bold
prophet. But how well the prophet was heard!
Down came the fire and devoured not only the
sacrifice, but the wood, the stones, and even
the very water that was in the trenches, for
Jehovah God had answered his servant's
prayer.

We sometimes may do the same and say to Him, "Oh, by your deity, by your existence, if indeed You are God, now show Yourself for the help of Your people!"

The Sufferings of Jesus

Lastly, the grand Christian argument is the sufferings, the death, the merit, the intercession of Christ Jesus. Friends, I am afraid we do not understand what we have at our command when we are allowed to plead with God for Christ's sake. I met with this thought the other day; it was somewhat new to me, but I believe it should not have been. When we ask God to hear us, pleading Christ's name, we usually mean, "O Lord, Your dear Son deserves this of You; do this for me because of what He merits." But if we knew it, we might go further. Suppose you should say to me, you who keep a warehouse in the city, "Sir, call at my office, and use my name, and say that they are to give you such a thing." I would go in and use your name, and I would obtain my request as a matter of right and a matter of necessity.

This is virtually what Jesus Christ says to us. "If you need anything from God, all that the Father has belongs to Me; go and use My name." Suppose that you give a man your checkbook signed with your own name and left blank, to be filled in as he chooses. That would be very close to what Jesus has done in these words, *"If ye shall ask any thing in my name, I will do it"* (John 14:14). If I had a good name at the bottom of the check, I would be sure that it would be cashed when I went to the bank with it. So when you have got Christ's name—to whom the very justice of God has become a debtor and whose merits have claims with the Most High—when you have Christ's name, there is no need to speak with fear and trembling and bated breath. Oh, waver not, and let not faith stagger! When you plead the name of Christ, you plead that which shakes the gates of hell and that which the hosts of heaven obey, and God Himself feels the sacred power of that divine plea.

Friends, you would do better if you sometimes thought more in your prayers of Christ's griefs and groans. Bring before the Lord His wounds; tell the Lord of His cries; make the groans of Jesus cry again from Gethsemane; and make His blood speak again from that frozen Calvary. Speak out and tell the Lord that with such griefs and cries and groans to plead, you cannot take a denial. Such arguments as these will aid you.

A Mouth Filled with Praises

If the Holy Spirit will teach us how to order our cause and how to fill our mouths with arguments, the result will be that we will have our mouths filled with praises. The man who has his mouth full of arguments in prayer will soon have his mouth full of benedictions in answer to prayer.

Dear friend, you have your mouth full right now, have you? What of? Full of complaining? Pray to the Lord to rinse that black stuff out of your mouth, for it will little help you, and it will be bitter in your bowels one of these days.

Oh, have your mouth full of prayer, full of it, full of arguments, so that there is room for nothing else. Then come with this blessed mouthful, and you will soon go away with whatever you have asked of God. Only *"delight thyself also in the LORD; and he shall give thee the desires of thine heart"* (Ps. 37:4).

It is said—I do not know how true it is—that the explanation of the text, *"Open thy mouth wide, and I will fill it"* (Ps. 81:10), may be found in a very singular Oriental custom. It is said that not many years ago—I remember the circumstance being reported—the King of Persia ordered the chief of his nobility, who had done something or other that had greatly gratified him, to open his mouth. When he had done so, he began to put into his mouth pearls, diamonds, rubies, and emeralds, until he had filled it with as much as it could hold, and then he bade him go his way. This is said to have been occasionally done in Oriental courts toward great favorites.

Now, certainly whether that is an explanation of the text or not, it is an illustration of it. God says, "Open your mouth with arguments," and then He will fill it with priceless mercies, gems unspeakably valuable. Would a man not open his mouth wide when he could have it filled in such a style? Surely the most simpleminded among you would be wise enough for that. Oh, let us then open wide our mouths when we plead with God. Our needs are great, let our askings be great, and the supply will be great, too. *"Ye are not straitened in* [Him], *but ye are straitened in your own bowels"* (2 Cor. 6:12). May the Lord give you large-mouthedness in prayer and great potency, not in the use of language, but in employing arguments.

What I have been speaking to the Christian is applicable in great measure to the unconverted man. May God grant you to see the force of it and to fly in humble prayer to the

Lord Jesus Christ and to find eternal life in Him.

Chapter Four

Pleading

But I am poor and needy: make haste unto me,
O God: thou art my help and my deliverer;
O LORD, make no tarrying.
—Psalm 70:5

Young painters were eager in the olden times to study under the great masters. They concluded that they would more easily attain excellence if they entered the schools of eminent men. Men have paid large premiums so that their sons may be apprenticed to those who best understood their trades or professions.

Now, if any of us would learn the sacred art and mystery of prayer, it is well for us to study the productions of the greatest masters of that science. I am unable to point out one who understood it better than the psalmist David. So well did he know how to praise that his psalms have become the language of good men in all ages. So well did he understand how to pray that if we catch his spirit and follow his mode of prayer, we will have learned to plead with God after the most powerful sort. Place before you, first of all, David's Son and David's Lord, that most mighty of all intercessors, and, next to Him, you will find David to be one of the most admirable models for your imitation.

We will consider our text, then, as one of the productions of a great master in spiritual matters. We will study it, praying all the while that God will help us to pray in the same fashion.

In our text we find four aspects of the soul of a successful pleader: First, we view the soul confessing, for he says, *"I am poor and needy."* Next, you have the soul pleading, for he makes a plea out of his poor condition and adds, *"Make haste unto me, O God!"* Third, you see a soul in its urgency, for he cries, *"Make haste,"* and he varies the expression but keeps the same idea: *"Make no tarrying."* And you have, in the fourth and last view, a soul grasping God, for the psalmist puts it this way: *"Thou art my help and my deliverer."* With both hands he lays hold upon His God, so as not to let Him go until a blessing is obtained.

A Soul Confessing

To begin with, then, we see in this model of supplication a soul confessing. The wrestler strips before he enters the contest, and confession does the same for the man who is about to plead with God. A racer on the plains of prayer cannot hope to win unless, by confession, repentance, and faith, he lays aside every weight of sin. (See Hebrews 12:1.)

Now, let it be ever remembered that confession is absolutely necessary to the sinner when he first seeks a Savior. It is not possible for you, seeker, to obtain peace for your troubled heart until you have acknowledged your transgression and your iniquity before the Lord. You may do what you will, yes, even attempt to believe in Jesus, but you will find that the faith of God's elect is not in you unless you are willing to make a full confession of your transgression and lay bare your heart before God.

Usually, we do not give charity to those who do not acknowledge that they need it: the physician does not send his medicine to those who are not sick. The blind man in the Gospels had to feel his blindness and to sit by the wayside begging; if he had entertained a doubt as to whether he were blind or not, the Lord would have passed him by. He opens the eyes of those who confess their blindness, but of others He says, "[Because] *ye say, We see; therefore your sin remaineth*" (John 9:41). He asks of those who are brought to Him, *"What wilt thou that I should do unto thee?"* (Mark 10:51) in order that their need may be publicly avowed. It must be so with all of us; we must offer the confession, or we cannot gain the blessing.

Let me speak especially to you who desire to find peace with God and salvation through the precious blood: you will do well to make your confession before God very frank, very sincere, very explicit. Surely you have nothing to hide, for there is nothing that you can hide. He knows your guilt already, but He would have you know it; therefore, He bids you to confess it. Go into the details of your sin in your secret acknowledgments before God. Strip yourself of all excuses; make no apologies. Say,

Against thee, thee only, have I sinned, and done this evil in thy sight: that thou mightest be justified when thou speakest, and be clear when thou judgest. (Ps. 51:4)

Acknowledge the evil of sin; ask God to make you feel it. Do not treat it as a trifle, for it is none. To redeem the sinner from the effects of sin, Christ Himself had to die; and unless you are delivered from it, you must die eternally. Therefore, do not play with sin. Do not confess it as though it were some venial fault that would not have been noticed unless God had been too severe; but labor to see sin as God sees it, as an offense against all that is good, a rebellion against all that is kind. See it to be treason, to be ingratitude, to be a low and base thing.

Never expect that the King of heaven will pardon a traitor if he will not confess and forsake his treason. Even the tenderest father expects the child to humble himself when he has offended, and he will not withdraw his frown from him until with tears the child has said, "Father, I have sinned."

Do you dare expect God to humble Himself to you, and would it not be so if He did not constrain you to humble yourself to Him? Would you have Him ignore your faults and wink at your transgressions? He will have mercy, but He must be holy. He is ready to forgive but not to tolerate sin. Therefore, He cannot let you be forgiven if you hug your sins or if you presume to say, "I have not sinned." Hasten, then, seeker; hasten, I pray you, to the mercy seat with this upon your lips: *"'I am poor and needy,'* I am sinful, and I am lost; have pity on me." With such an acknowledgment you begin your prayer well, and through Jesus you shall prosper in it.

Beloved friends, the same principle applies to the church of God. If you are praying for a display of the Holy Spirit's power in your church, in order to have successful pleading in this matter, it is necessary that you unanimously make the confession of our text, *"I am poor and needy."* We must admit that we are powerless in this business. Salvation is of the Lord, and we cannot save a single soul. The Spirit of God is treasured up in Christ, and we must seek the Spirit of the great Head of the church. We cannot command the Spirit, and yet we can do nothing without Him. He *"bloweth where* [He] *listeth"* (John 3:8). We must deeply feel and honestly acknowledge this. Before God blesses His church, He will make it know that the blessing is altogether from Himself. *"Not by might, nor by power, but by my spirit, saith the LORD of hosts"* (Zech. 4:6).

The career of Gideon was a very remarkable one, and it commenced with two most instructive signs. (See Judges 6:36–40.) I think our heavenly Father would have all of us learn the very same lesson that He taught to Gideon, and when we have mastered that lesson, He will use us for His own purposes. You remember Gideon laid a fleece on the barn floor; and in the morning all around was dry, and the fleece alone was wet. God alone had saturated the fleece so that he could wring it out; and its moisture was not due to its being placed in a favorable situation, for all around was dry.

He would have us learn that if the dew of His grace fills any one of us with its heavenly moisture, it is not because we lie on the barn floor of a ministry that God usually blesses or because we are in a church that the Lord graciously visits. Rather, the visitations of His Spirit are fruits of the Lord's sovereign grace and gifts of His infinite love, not of the will of man nor by man.

But then the miracle was reversed, for, as old Thomas Fuller says, "God's miracles will bear to be turned inside out and will look as glorious one way as another." The next night the fleece was dry and all around was wet, for skeptics might have said, "Yes, but a fleece would naturally attract moisture, and if there were any in the air, it would likely be absorbed by the wool." But, lo, on this occasion, the dew is not where it might be expected to be, even though it lies thickly all around. Damp is the stone, and dry is the fleece.

So, God will have us know that He does not give us His grace because of any natural adaptation in us to receive it. Even where He has given a preparedness of heart to receive, He will have us understand that His grace and His Spirit are free in action and sovereign in operation; He is not bound to work after any rule of our making. If the fleece is wet, He makes it wet, and not because it is a fleece, but because He chooses to do so. He will have all the glory of all His grace from first to last.

Come then, my friends, and become disciples of this truth. Consider that from the great Father of lights every good and perfect gift must come (James 1:17). *"We are his workmanship"* (Eph. 2:10); He must work all our works in us. Grace is not to be commanded by our position or condition: *"the wind bloweth where it listeth"* (John 3:8). The Lord works, and no man can hinder. But if He works not, the mightiest and the most zealous will labor in vain (Ps. 127:1).

It is very significant that before Christ fed the thousands, He made the disciples sum up all their provisions. It was good to let them see how low the food supply had become, for then when the crowds were fed, they could not say that the basket fed them or that the lad had done it. God will make us feel that our barley loaves are very little and our fishes are very small, and He will compel us to ask, *"What are they among so many?"* (John 6:9).

When the Savior bade His disciples to cast the net on the right side of the ship and they dragged such a mighty catch to land, He did not work the miracle until they had confessed that they had toiled all night and had caught nothing. They were thus taught that the success of their fishery was dependent upon the Lord and that it was neither their nets nor the way of dragging them nor their skill and art in handling their vessels, but that altogether and entirely their success came from their Lord. We must get down to this, and the sooner we come to it the better.

Immediately preceding the ancient Jews' keeping of the yearly Passover, observe what they did. The unleavened bread was to be brought in, and the paschal lamb to be eaten; but there was to be no unleavened bread and no paschal lamb until they had purged out the old leaven. If you have any old strength and self-confidence, if you have anything that is your own and is, therefore, leavened, it must be swept right out. There must be a bare cupboard before there can come in the heavenly provision upon which the spiritual passover can be kept.

I thank God when He cleans us out. I bless His name when He brings us to feel our soul poverty as a church, for then the blessing will be sure to come.

One other illustration will show this, perhaps, more distinctly still. Behold Elijah with the priests of Baal at Carmel. The test appointed to decide Israel's choice was this: *"The God that answereth by fire, let him be God"* (1 Kings 18:24). Baal's priests invoked the heavenly flame in vain. Elijah is confident that it will come upon his sacrifice, but he is sternly resolved that the false priests and the fickle people should not imagine that he himself had produced the fire. He determines to make it clear that there is no human contrivance, trickery, or maneuver about the matter. The flame should be seen to be of the Lord, and of the Lord alone. Remember the stern prophet's commands:

> *Fill four barrels with water, and pour it on the burnt sacrifice, and on the wood. And he said, Do it the second time. And they did it the second time. And he said, Do it the third time. And they did it the third time. And the water ran round about the altar; and he filled the trench also with water.* (1 Kings 18:33–35)

There could be no latent fires there. If there had been any combustibles or chemicals calculated to produce fire after the manner of the cheats of the time, they would all have been dampened and spoiled.

When no one could imagine that man could burn the sacrifice, then the prophet lifted up his eyes to heaven and began to plead, and down came the fire of the Lord. It consumed the burnt sacrifice and the wood, as well as the altar stones and the dust, and even licked up the water that was in the trench. Then when all the people saw it, they fell on their faces, and they said, "Jehovah is the God; Jehovah is the God."

The Lord, if He means to bless us greatly, may send us the trial of pouring on the water once, twice, and three times. He may discourage us, grieve us, try us, and bring us low, until all will see that it is not of the preacher, it is not of the organization, it is not of man, but altogether of God, the Alpha and the Omega, *"who worketh all things after the counsel of his own will"* (Eph. 1:11).

Thus I have shown you that for a successful season of prayer, the best beginning is a confession that we are poor and needy.

A Soul Pleading

Secondly, after the soul has unburdened itself of all weights of merit and self-sufficiency, it proceeds to prayer, and we have before us a soul pleading. *"I am poor and needy: make haste unto me, O God: thou art my help and my deliverer; O LORD, make no tarrying."* The careful reader will perceive four pleas in this single verse.

Upon this topic I would remark that it is the habit of faith, when it is praying, to use pleas. Mere prayer sayers, who do not pray at all, forget to argue with God; however, those who would prevail bring forth their reasons and their strong arguments, and they debate the question with the Lord. They who play at wrestling catch here and there at random, but those who are really wrestling have a certain way of grasping the opponent—a certain mode of throwing and the like. They work according to order and rule. Faith's art of wrestling is to plead with God and say with boldness, "Let it be thus and thus, for these reasons."

Hosea tells us of Jacob at Jabbok, that *"there he spake with us"* (Hos. 12:4); from this I understand that Jacob instructed us by his example. Now, the two pleas that Jacob used were God's precept and God's promise. First, he said, "[Thou] *saidst unto me, Return unto thy country, and to thy kindred"* (Gen. 32:9). He as much put it this way: "Lord, I am in difficulty, but I have come here through obedience to You. You told me to do this. Now, since You commanded me to come here, into the very teeth of my brother Esau, who comes to meet me like a lion, Lord, You cannot be so unfaithful as to bring me into danger and then leave me in it." This was sound reasoning, and it prevailed with God.

Then Jacob also urged a promise: *"Thou saidst, I will surely do thee good"* (Gen. 32:12). Among men, it is a masterly way of reasoning when you can challenge your opponent with his own words. You may quote other authorities, and he may say, "I deny their force"; but when you quote a man against himself, you foil him completely. When you bring a man's promise to his mind, he must either confess himself to be unfaithful and changeable, or, if he holds to being the same and being true to his word, you have him, and you have won your will of him.

Oh, friends, let us learn to plead the precepts, the promises, and whatever else may serve our case; but let us always have something to plead. Do not reckon you have prayed unless you have pleaded, for pleading is the very marrow of prayer. He who pleads well knows the secret of prevailing with God, especially if he pleads the blood of Jesus, for that unlocks the treasury of heaven. Many keys fit many locks, but the master key is the blood and the name of Him who died but rose again and ever lives in heaven to save to the uttermost. Faith's pleas are plentiful, and this is well, for faith is placed in various positions and needs them all.

Faith will boldly plead all God's gracious relationships. It will say to Him, "Are You not the Creator? Will You forsake the work of Your own hands? Are You not the Redeemer? You have redeemed Your servant; will You cast me away?" Faith usually delights to lay hold upon the fatherhood of God. This is generally one of its master points; when it brings this into the field, it wins the day. "You are a Father, and would You chasten us as though You would kill? A Father, and will You not provide? A Father, and have You no sympathy and no bowels of compassion? A Father, and can You deny what Your own child asks of You?" Whenever I am impressed with the divine majesty and so, perhaps, a little dispirited in prayer, I find that the short and sweet remedy is to remember that, although He is a great King and infinitely glorious, I am His child; and no matter who the father is, the child may always be bold with his father. Yes, faith can plead any and all of the relationships in which God stands to His chosen.

Pleading

Faith, too, can ply heaven with the divine promises. Suppose you went to a bank and saw a man go in and out and lay a piece of paper on the table and pick it up again and nothing more. If he did that several times a day, I think there would soon be orders issued to the porter to keep the man out because he was merely wasting the clerk's time and doing nothing purposeful. Those men who come to the bank in earnest present their checks, they wait until they receive their money, and then they go but not without having transacted real business. They do not put the paper down, speak about the excellent signature, and discuss the correctness of the document; they want their money for it, and they are not content without it. These are the people who are always welcome at the bank and not the triflers.

Alas, a great many people play at praying; it is nothing better. I say they play at praying; they do not expect God to give them an answer, and thus they are mere triflers, who mock the Lord. He who prays in a business-like way, meaning what he says, honors the Lord. The Lord does not play at promising; Jesus did not sport at confirming the word by His blood; and we must not make a jest of prayer by going about it in a listless, unexpecting spirit.

The Holy Spirit is in earnest, and we must also be in earnest. We must go for a blessing and not be satisfied until we have it, like the hunter who is not satisfied because he has run so many miles but is never content until he takes his prey.

Faith, moreover, pleads the performances of God; it looks back on the past and says, "Lord, You delivered me on such and such an occasion; will You fail me now?" It, moreover, takes its life as a whole and pleads thus:

> After so much mercy past,
>   Wilt thou let me sink at last?

"Have you brought me this far so that I may be put to shame at the end?" Faith knows how to bring out the ancient mercies of God, and it makes them arguments for present favors. But your time would all be gone if I tried to exhibit even a thousandth part of faith's pleas.

Sometimes, however, faith's pleas are very singular, as in this text. It is by no means according to the proud rule of human nature to plead, *"I am poor and needy: make haste unto me, O God."* It is like another prayer of David: *"Pardon mine iniquity; for it is great"* (Ps. 25:11). It is not the manner of men to plead this way; they say, "Lord, have mercy on me, for I am not so bad a sinner as some." But faith reads things in a truer light and bases its pleas on truth. "Lord, because my sin is great and You are a great God, let Your great mercy be magnified in me."

You know the story of the Syrophenician woman; that is a grand instance of the ingenuity of faith's reasoning. (See Matthew 15:22–28.) She came to Christ about her daughter, and He answered her not a word. What do you think her heart said? Why, she said in herself, "It is well, for He has not denied me. Since He has not spoken at all, He has not refused me." With this for an encouragement, she began to plead again. Soon Christ spoke to her sharply, and then her brave heart said, "I have gained words from Him at last; I will have deeds from Him by and by." That also cheered her. Then, when He called her a dog, "Ah," she reasoned, "but a dog is a part of the family; it has some connection with the master of the house. Though it does not eat meat from the table, it gets the crumbs under it, and so I have You now, great Master, dog as I am. The great mercy that I ask of You, great as it is to me, is only a crumb to You. Grant it then, I beseech You." Could she fail to have her request? Impossible! When faith has a will, it always finds a way, and it will win the day when all things forebode defeat.

Faith's pleas are singular, but, let me add, faith's pleas are always sound. After all, it is a very telling plea to urge that we are poor and needy. Is that not the main argument with mercy? Necessity is the very best plea with benevolence, either human or divine. Is not our need the best reason we can urge? If we would have a physician come quickly to a sick man, "Sir," we say, "it is no common case; he is on the point of death. Come to him; come quickly!" If we wanted our city firemen to rush to a fire, we would not say to them, "Make haste, for it is only a small fire." On the contrary, we urge that it is an old house, full of combustible materials, and there are rumors of petroleum and gunpowder on the premises. Besides, it is near a timber yard, hosts of wooden cottages are close by, and before long we will have half the city in a blaze. We put the case in as bad a light as we can. Oh, for wisdom to be equally wise in pleading with God, to find arguments everywhere but especially to find them in our necessities!

They said two centuries ago that the trade of beggary was the easiest one to carry on but that it paid the worst. I am not sure about the latter at this time, but certainly the trade of begging with God is a hard one, and undoubtedly it pays the best of anything in the world. It is very noteworthy that beggars with men usually have plenty of pleas on hand. When a man is driven hard and starving, he can usually find a reason why he should ask aid of every likely person. Suppose it is a person to whom he is already under many obligations; then the poor creature reasons, "I may safely ask of him again, for he knows me and has always been very kind." If he never asked of the person before, then he says, "I have never worried him before; he cannot say he has already done all he can for me. I will be bold to begin with him." If it is one of his own kin, then he says, "Surely you will help me in my distress, for you are a relative." And if it is a stranger, he says, "I have often found strangers kinder than my own blood; help me, I entreat you." If he asks of the rich, he pleads that they will never miss what they give. If he begs of the poor, he urges that they know what want means, and he is sure they will sympathize with him in his great distress.

Oh, that we were half as much on the alert to fill our mouths with arguments when we are before the Lord! How is it that we are not half awake and do not seem to have any spiritual senses aroused? May God grant that we may learn the art of pleading with the eternal God, for by that we will prevail with Him through the merit of Jesus Christ.

An Urgent Soul

I must be brief on the next point, which is having an urgency in our souls: *"Make haste unto me, O God...O LORD, make no tarrying."* We may well be urgent with God if we are not yet saved, for our need is urgent. We are in constant peril, and the peril is of the most tremendous kind. O sinner, within an hour, within a minute, you may be where hope can never visit you; therefore, cry, "Make haste, O God, to deliver me; make haste to help me, O Lord!" Yours is not a case that can bear lingering; you do not have time to procrastinate. Therefore, be urgent, for your need is so.

Remember, if you really are under a sense of need and the Spirit of God is at work within you, you will and must be urgent. An ordinary sinner may be content to wait, but a quickened sinner wants mercy now. A dead sinner will lie quiet, but a living sinner cannot rest until pardon is sealed home to his soul. If you are urgent, I am glad of it, because your urgency, I trust, arises from the possession of spiritual life. When you can live no longer without a

Savior, the Savior will come to you, and you will rejoice in Him.

Believer, the same truth holds true with you. God will come to bless you, and come speedily, when your sense of need becomes deep and urgent. Oh, how great is the church's need! We will grow cold, unholy, and worldly; there will be no conversions; there will be no additions to our numbers; there will be subtractions; there will be divisions; there will be mischief of all kinds; Satan will rejoice; and Christ will be dishonored, unless we obtain a larger measure of the Holy Spirit. Our need is urgent, and when we feel that need thoroughly, then we will get the blessing that we want.

For my part, brothers and sisters, I desire to feel a spirit of urgency within my soul as I plead with God for the dew of His grace to descend upon the church. I am not bashful in this matter, for I have a license to pray. Begging is forbidden in the streets, but before the Lord I am a licensed beggar. The Bible says, *"Men ought always to pray, and not to faint"* (Luke 18:1). You land on the shores of a foreign country with the greatest confidence when you carry a passport with you, and God has issued passports to His children by which they come boldly to His mercy seat. He has invited you,

He has encouraged you, He has bidden you to come to Him, and He has promised that *"whatsoever ye shall ask in prayer, believing, ye shall receive"* (Matt. 21:22). Come, then; come urgently; come persistently; come with this plea, *"I am poor and needy...O LORD, make no tarrying."* Then a blessing will surely come; it will not tarry. God grant that we may see it and give Him the glory of it.

The Soul Grasping God

I am sorry to have been so brief where I needed to enlarge, but I must close with the fourth point. Here is another part of the art and mystery of prayer—the soul grasping God. It has pleaded, and it has been urgent, but now it comes to close quarters. It grasps the covenant angel with one hand, *"Thou art my help,"* and with the other, *"Thou art...my deliverer."* Oh, those blessed *my*'s, those potent *my*'s. The sweetness of the Bible lies in the possessive pronouns, and he who is taught to use them as the psalmist did will be a conqueror with the eternal God.

Now, sinner, I pray that you may be helped to say to the blessed Christ of God, *"Thou art my help and my deliverer."* Perhaps you mourn that you cannot get that length, but, poor soul, have you any other help? If you have, then you cannot hold two helpers with the same hand. "Oh, no," you say, "I have no help anywhere. I have no hope except in Christ." Well, then, poor soul, since your hand is empty, that empty hand was made on purpose to grasp your Lord with. Lay hold on Him! Say to Him this day, "Lord, I will hang on You as poor, lame Jacob did. Now I cannot help myself; I will cleave to You. *'I will not let thee go, except thou bless me'* (Gen. 32:26)."

"Ah, it would be too bold," says one. But the Lord loves holy boldness in poor sinners; He would have you be bolder than you think of being. It is an unhallowed bashfulness that dares not trust a crucified Savior. He died on purpose to save such as you are; let Him have His way with you, and do trust Him.

"Oh," says one, "but I am so unworthy." He came to seek and save the unworthy. He is not the Savior of the self-righteous; he is the sinners' Savior. *"Friend of...sinners"* (Matt. 11:19) is His name. Unworthy one, lay hold on Him!

"Oh," says one, "but I have no right." Well, since you have no right, your need will be your claim; it is all the claim you need.

I think I hear one say, "It is too late for me to plead for grace." It cannot be; it is impossible. While you live and desire mercy, it is not too late to seek it. Notice the parable of the man who wanted three loaves. (See Luke 11:5–8.) I will tell you what crossed my mind when I read it. The man went to his friend at midnight. It could not have been later. If it had been a little later than midnight, it would have been early the next morning, and so not late at all. It was midnight, and it could not have been later. So, if it is downright midnight with your soul, yet, be of good cheer. Jesus is an out-of-season Savior. Many of His servants are *"born out of due time"* (1 Cor. 15:8).

Any season is the right season to call upon the name of Jesus; therefore, do not let the Devil tempt you with the thought that it can be too late. Go to Jesus now, go at once, and lay hold on the horns of the altar by a venturesome faith. Say, "Sacrifice for sinners, You are a sacrifice for me. Intercessor for the graceless, You are an intercessor for me. You who distributes gifts to the rebellious, distribute gifts to me, for a rebel I have been. *'When we were yet without strength, in due time Christ died for the ungodly'* (Rom. 5:6). Such am I, Master; let the power of Your death be seen in me to save my soul."

Oh, you that are saved and, therefore, love Christ, I want you, dear friends, as the saints of God, to practice this last part of my subject and be sure to lay hold upon God in prayer. *"Thou art my help and my deliverer."* As a church we throw ourselves upon the strength of God, and we can do nothing without Him. But we do not mean to be without Him; we will hold Him fast. *"Thou art my help and my deliverer."*

There was a boy in Athens, according to the old story, who used to boast that he ruled all of Athens. When they asked him how, he said, "Why, I rule my mother, my mother rules my father, and my father rules the city."

He who knows how to be master of prayer will rule the heart of Christ, and Christ can and will do all things for His people, for the Father has *"given all things into his hands"* (John 13:3). You can be omnipotent if you know how to pray, omnipotent in all things that glorify God. What does the Word itself say? *"Let him take hold of my strength"* (Isa. 27:5). Prayer moves the arm that moves the world. Oh, for grace to grasp almighty love in this fashion.

We want more holdfast prayer, more tugging and gripping and wrestling that says, *"I will not let thee go"* (Gen. 32:26). That picture of Jacob at Jabbok will suffice for us to close with. The covenant angel is there, and Jacob wants a blessing from him. He seems to put him off, but no put-offs will do for Jacob. Then the angel endeavors to escape from him, and he tugs and strives; this he may do, but no efforts will make Jacob relax his grasp. At last, the angel falls from ordinary wrestling to wounding him in the very seat of his strength. Jacob will let his thigh go, and all his limbs go, but he will not let the angel go. The poor man's strength shrivels under the withering touch, but in his weakness he is still strong. He throws his arms around the mysterious man, and he holds him as in a death grip.

Then the other says, *"Let me go, for the day breaketh"* (Gen. 32:26). Note, he did not shake him off; he only said, *"Let me go."* The angel will do nothing to force him to relax his hold; he leaves that to his voluntary will.

The valiant Jacob cries, "No, I am set on it. I am resolved to win an answer to my prayer. *'I will not let thee go, except thou bless me'* (Gen. 32:26)."

Now, when the church begins to pray, it may be at first that the Lord will act as though he would go further (see Luke 24:28), and we may fear that no answer will be given. Hold on, dear friends. *"Be ye stedfast, unmoveable"* (1 Cor. 15:58), despite all. By and by, it may be, there will come discouragements where we looked for a flowing success. We will find friends hindering; some will be slumbering and others sinning. Backsliders and impenitent souls will abound. But let us not be turned aside. Let us be all the more eager.

And if it should so happen that we ourselves become distressed and dispirited and we feel we never were so weak as we are now, never mind, friends; still hold on. For when the sinew is shrunk, the victory is near. Grasp with a tighter grip than ever. Let this be our resolution, *"I will not let thee go, except thou bless me"* (Gen. 32:26). Remember, the longer the blessing is in coming, the richer it will be when it arrives. That which is gained speedily by a single prayer is sometimes only a second-rate blessing; but that which is gained after many a desperate tug, and many an awful struggle, is a full-weighted and precious blessing.

The children of persistence are always fair to look upon. The blessing that costs us the most prayer will be worth the most. Only let us be persevering in supplication, and we will gain a broad, far-reaching blessing for ourselves, the churches, and the world. I wish it were in my power to stir you all to fervent prayer, but I must leave it with the great Author of all true supplication, namely, the

Holy Spirit. May He work in us mightily, for Jesus' sake. Amen.

Chapter Five

The Throne of Grace

The throne of grace.
—Hebrews 4:16

These words are found embedded in that gracious verse, *"Let us therefore come boldly unto the throne of grace, that we may obtain mercy, and find grace to help in time of need"* (Heb. 4:16). They are a gem in a golden setting. True prayer is an approach of the soul by the Spirit of God to the throne of God. It is not the utterance of words; it is not alone the feeling of desires; but it is the advance of the desires to God, the spiritual approach of our nature towards the Lord our God. True prayer is neither a mere mental exercise nor a vocal performance. It is far deeper than that. It is spiritual commerce with the Creator of heaven and earth.

God is a Spirit, unseen by mortal eye and only to be perceived by the inner man. Our spirit within us, begotten by the Holy Spirit at our regeneration, discerns the Great Spirit, communes with Him, sets before Him its requests, and receives from Him answers of peace. It is a spiritual business from beginning to end. Its aim and objective end not with man, but they reach to God Himself.

In order to offer such prayer, the work of the Holy Spirit Himself is needed. If prayer were of the lips alone, we would only need breath in our nostrils to pray. If prayer were of the desires alone, many excellent desires are easily felt, even by natural men. But when it is the spiritual desire and the spiritual fellowship of the human spirit with the Great Spirit, then the Holy Spirit Himself must be present all through it. He helps infirmity and gives life and power. Without the Holy Spirit, true prayer will never be presented; the thing offered to God will wear the name and have the form, but the inner life of prayer will be far from it.

Moreover, it is clear from the connection of our text that the interposition of the Lord Jesus Christ is essential to acceptable prayer. As prayer will not be truly prayer without the Spirit of God, so it will not be prevailing prayer without the Son of God. He, the Great High Priest, must go within the veil for us; no, through His crucified person the veil must be entirely taken away. Until then, we are shut out from the living God. The man who, despite the teaching of Scripture, tries to pray without our Savior, insults the Deity. He who imagines that his own natural desires, coming up before God, unsprinkled with the precious blood, will be an acceptable sacrifice before God, makes a mistake; he has not brought an offering that God can accept, any more than if he had struck off a dog's head or offered an unclean sacrifice. Worked in us by the Spirit, presented for us by the Christ of God, prayer becomes power before the Most High, but not by any other way.

In trying to write about the text, I will outline it this way: First, here is a throne. Second, here is grace. Then we will put the two together, and we will see grace on a throne. And putting them together in another order, we will see sovereignty manifesting itself and resplendent in grace.

A Throne

Our text speaks of a throne, *"the throne of grace."* God is to be viewed in prayer as our Father; that is the aspect that is dearest to us. However, we are not to regard Him as though He were such as we are. Our Savior has qualified the expression *"our Father"* with the words *"which art in heaven"* (Matt. 6:9) close at the heels of that gracious name. He wanted to remind us that our Father is still infinitely greater than we are. He has bidden us say, *"Hallowed be thy name. Thy kingdom come"* (Matt. 6:9–10), for our Father is still to be regarded as King. In prayer we come not only to our Father's feet, but also to the throne of the Great Monarch of the universe. The mercy seat is a throne, and we must not forget this.

Lowly Reverence

If prayer should always be regarded by us as an entrance into the courts of the Royalty of heaven, if we are to behave ourselves as courtiers should in the presence of an illustrious majesty, then we are not at a loss to know the right spirit in which to pray. If in prayer we come to a throne, it is clear that we should, in the first place, approach in a spirit of lowly reverence. It is expected that the subject in approaching the king should pay him homage and honor. The pride that will not acknowledge the king, the treason which rebels against the sovereign will, should, if it is wise, avoid any near approach to the throne. Let pride bite the curb at a distance, let treason lurk in corners, for only lowly reverence may come before the King Himself when He sits clothed in His robes of majesty.

In our case, the King before whom we come is the highest of all monarchs, the King of Kings, the Lord of Lords. Emperors are but the shadows of His imperial power. They call themselves kings by right divine, but what divine right do they have? Common sense laughs their pretensions to scorn. The Lord alone has divine right, and to Him only does the kingdom belong. He is *"the blessed and only Potentate"* (1 Tim. 6:15). They are but nominal kings, to be set up and put down at the will of men or the decree of providence; but He is Lord alone, the Prince of the kings of the earth.

> He sits on no precarious throne
> Nor borrows leave to be.

My heart, be sure that you prostrate yourself in such a presence. Since He is so great, place your mouth in the dust before Him, for He is the most powerful of all kings. His throne has sway in all worlds. Heaven obeys Him cheerfully, hell trembles at His frown, and earth is constrained to yield Him homage willingly or unwillingly. His power can make or can destroy. To create or to crush, either is easy enough to Him. My soul, be sure that when you draw nigh to the Omnipotent God, who is as a consuming fire, you put your shoes from off your feet and worship Him with lowliest humility.

Besides, He is the most holy of all kings. His throne is a great, white throne, unspotted and clear as crystal. *"The heavens are not clean in his sight"* (Job 15:15), and *"his angels he charged with folly"* (Job 4:18). And you, a sinful creature, with lowliness you should draw near to him. Familiarity there may be, but let it not be unhallowed. Boldness there should be, but let it not be impertinent. Still, you are on earth and He in heaven. Still, you are a worm of the dust, a creature *"crushed before the moth"* (Job 4:19), and He is the Everlasting. *"Before the mountains were brought forth... thou art God"* (Ps. 90:2). If all created things should pass away again, still He would be the same. My friends, I am afraid we do not bow as we should before the Eternal Majesty; but, henceforth, let us ask the Spirit of God to put us in a right attitude, so that every one of our prayers may be a reverential approach to the Infinite Majesty above.

Devout Joyfulness

A throne is, in the second place, to be approached with devout joyfulness. If I find myself favored by divine grace to stand among those favored ones who frequent His courts, should I not feel glad? I might have been in

His prison, but I am before His throne. I might have been driven from His presence forever, but I am permitted to come near to Him, even into His royal palace, into His secret chamber of gracious audience. Should I not then be thankful? Should not my thankfulness ascend into joy, and should I not feel that I am honored, that I am made the recipient of great favors, when I am permitted to pray?

Why is your countenance sad, oh, suppliant, when you stand before the throne of grace? If you were before the throne of justice to be condemned for your iniquities, you might well be sad. But now you are favored to come before the King in His silken robes of love; let your face shine with sacred delight. If your sorrows are heavy, tell them to Him, for He can comfort you. If your sins are multiplied, confess them, for He can forgive them. Oh, courtiers in the halls of such a Monarch, be exceedingly glad, and mingle praises with your prayers.

Complete Submission

It is a throne, and therefore, in the third place, whenever it is approached, it should be with complete submission. We do not pray to God to instruct Him as to what He ought to do;

neither for a moment must we presume to dictate the line of the divine procedure. We are permitted to say to God, "Thus and thus would we have it," but we must evermore add, "But, seeing that we are ignorant and may be mistaken—seeing that we are still in the flesh and, therefore, may be actuated by carnal motives—not as we will, but as You will."

Who would dictate to the throne? No loyal child of God will for a moment imagine that he is to occupy the place of the King, but he bows before Him who has a right to be Lord of all. Though he utters his desire earnestly, vehemently, persistently, and pleads and pleads again, yet it is evermore with this needful reservation: "Your will be done, my Lord; and if I ask anything that is not in accordance with Your will, my inmost will is that You would be good enough to deny Your servant. I will take it as a true answer if You refuse me if I ask that which does not seem good in Your sight." If we constantly remembered this, I think we would be less inclined to push certain suits before the throne, for we would feel, "I am here in seeking my own ease, my own comfort, my own advantage, and, perhaps, I may be asking for that which would dishonor God. Therefore, I will speak with the deepest submission to the divine decrees."

Enlarged Expectations

Friends, in the fourth place, if it is a throne, it ought to be approached with enlarged expectations. Well does our hymn put it:

> Thou art coming to a king:
> Large petitions with thee bring.

We do not come in prayer, as it were, only to God's poorhouse where He dispenses His favors to the poor, nor do we come to the back door of the house of mercy to receive the broken scraps, though that would be more than we deserve; to eat the crumbs that fall from the Master's table is more than we could claim. But, when we pray, we are standing in the palace on the glittering floor of the great King's own reception room, and thus we are placed upon a vantage ground. In prayer we stand where angels bow with veiled faces. There, even there, the cherubim and seraphim adore before that selfsame throne to which our prayers ascend. And should we come there with stunted requests and narrow and contracted faith? No, it does not become a King to be giving away pennies and nickels; He distributes pieces of gold. He scatters not, as poor men must, scraps of bread and broken meat, but He makes a feast of fat things, of fat things full of marrow, of wines well refined.

When Alexander's soldier was told to ask what he would, he did not ask sparingly after the nature of his own merits, but he made such a heavy demand that the royal treasurer refused to pay it and put the case to the king. Alexander, in right kingly sort, replied, "He knows how great Alexander is, and he has asked as from a king. Let him have what he requests." Take heed of imagining that God's thoughts are as your thoughts and His ways as your ways (Isa. 55:8). Do not bring before God small petitions and narrow desires and say, "Lord, do according to these." Remember, as high as the heavens are above the earth, so high are His ways above your ways, and His thoughts above your thoughts (Isa. 55:9). Ask, therefore, after a godlike sort. Ask for great things, for you are before a great throne. Oh, that we always felt this when we come before the throne of grace, for then He would do for us *exceeding abundantly above all that we ask or* [even] *think"* (Eph. 3:20).

Unstaggering Confidence

And, beloved, I may add, in the fifth place, that the right spirit in which to approach the throne of grace is that of unstaggering confidence. Who would doubt the King? Who dares impugn the Imperial word? It was well said that if integrity were banished from the hearts of all mankind besides, it ought still to dwell in the hearts of kings. Shame on a king if he can lie. The beggar in the streets is dishonored by a broken promise, but what can we say of a king if his word cannot be depended upon?

Oh, shame on us if we are unbelieving before the throne of the King of heaven and earth. With our God before us in all His glory, sitting on the throne of grace, will our hearts dare to say we mistrust Him? Will we imagine either that He cannot or will not keep His promise? There, surely, is the place for the child to trust his father, for the loyal subject to trust his monarch; therefore, all wavering or suspicion should be far from the throne. Unstaggering faith should be predominant before the mercy seat.

Deepest Sincerity

I have only one more remark to make on this point: if prayer is a coming before the throne of God, it ought to always be conducted with the deepest sincerity and in the spirit that makes everything *real*. If you are disloyal enough to despise the King, at least, for your own sake, do not mock Him to His face and when He is upon His throne. If anywhere you dare repeat holy words without heart, let it not be in Jehovah's palace. If I am called upon to pray in public, I must not dare use words that are intended to please the ears of my fellow-worshipers, but I must realize that I am speaking to God Himself and that I have business to transact with the great Lord. And, in my private prayer, if I rise from my bed in the morning and bow my knee and repeat certain words, or if go through the same regular form when I retire to rest at night, I rather sin than do anything that is good, unless my very soul speaks unto the Most High. Do you think that the King of heaven is delighted to hear you pronounce words with a frivolous tongue and a thoughtless mind? You know Him not. *"God is a Spirit: and they that worship him must worship him in spirit and in truth"* (John 4:24).

Beloved, the summary of all our remarks is just this: prayer is no trifle. It is an eminent and elevated act. It is a high and wondrous privilege. Under the old Persian Empire a few of the nobility were permitted at any time to come in to the king, and this was thought to be the highest privilege possessed by mortals. You and I, the people of God, have a permit, a passport, to come before the throne of heaven at any time we will, and we are encouraged to come there with great boldness. Still, let us not forget that it is no light thing to be a courtier in the courts of heaven and earth, to worship Him who made us and sustains us in being. Truly, when we attempt to pray, we may hear the voice saying out of the excellent glory, "Bow the knee." From all the spirits that behold the face of our Father who is in heaven, even now, I hear a voice that says,

> *O come, let us worship and bow down:*
> *let us kneel before the LORD our maker.*
> *For he is our God; and we are the people*
> *of his pasture, and the sheep of his*
> *hand.* (Ps. 95:6–7)

And, *"worship the LORD in the beauty of holiness. Fear before him, all the earth"* (1 Chron. 16:29–30).

Grace

Lest the glow and brilliance of the word *throne* should be too much for mortal vision, our text now presents us with the soft, gentle radiance of that delightful word *grace*. We are called to the throne of grace, not to the throne of law. Rocky Sinai once was the throne of law when God came to Paran with ten thousand of His holy ones. Who desired to draw near to that throne? Even Israel did not. Boundaries were set around the mount, and if even a beast touched the mount, it was stoned or thrust through with a dart. Oh, self-righteous ones who hope that you can obey the law and think that you can be saved by it, look to the flames that Moses saw, and shrink, and tremble, and despair. To that throne we do not come now, for through Jesus the case is changed. To a conscience purged by the precious blood, there is no anger upon the divine throne, though to our troubled minds:

> Once 'twas a seat of burning wrath,
> And shot devouring flame;
> Our God appeared consuming fire,
> And *jealous* was his name.

And, blessed be God, I am not now going to write about the throne of ultimate justice. Before that we will all come, and those of us who have believed will find it to be a throne of grace as well as of justice; for He who sits upon that throne will pronounce no sentence of condemnation against the man who is justified by faith. It is a throne set up on purpose for the dispensation of grace, a throne from which every utterance is an utterance of grace. The scepter that is stretched out from it is the silver scepter of grace. The decrees proclaimed from it are purposes of grace. The gifts that are scattered down its golden steps are gifts of grace. He who sits upon the throne is grace itself. It is *"the throne of grace"* to which we approach when we pray; let us think this over for a moment or two, by way of consolatory encouragement to those who are beginning to pray—indeed, to all of us who are praying men and women.

Faults Overlooked

If in prayer I come before a throne of grace, then the many faults of my prayer will be overlooked. In beginning to pray, dear friends, you feel as if you did not pray. The groanings of your spirit, when you rise from your knees, are such that you think there is nothing in them. What a blotted, blurred, smeared prayer it is. Never mind. You have not come to the throne of justice, or else when God perceived the fault in the prayer, He would spurn it. Your broken words, your gaspings, your stammerings, are before a throne of grace.

When any one of us has presented his best prayer before God, if he saw it as God sees it, there is no doubt he would make great lamentation over it. There is enough sin in the best prayer that was ever prayed to secure its being cast away from God. But it is not a throne of justice, I say again, and here is the hope for our lame, limping supplications. Our gracious King does not maintain a stately etiquette in His court like that which has been observed by princes among men, where a little mistake or a flaw would secure the petitioner's being dismissed with disgrace. Oh, no. The faulty cries of His children are not severely criticized by Him. The Lord High Chamberlain of the palace above, our Lord Jesus Christ, takes care to alter and amend every prayer before He presents it, and He makes the prayer perfect with His perfection and prevailing with His own merits. God looks upon the prayer as presented through Christ, and He forgives all of its own inherent faultiness.

How this ought to encourage any of us who feel ourselves to be feeble, wandering, and unskillful in prayer! If you cannot plead with God as sometimes you did in years gone by, if you feel as if somehow or other you have grown rusty in the work of supplication, never give up, but come still, yes, and come oftener.

For it is not a throne of severe criticism; it is a throne of grace to which you come.

Then, further, inasmuch as it is a throne of grace, the faults of the petitioner himself will not prevent the success of his prayer. Oh, what faults there are in us! To come before a throne, how unfit we are—we, that are all defiled with sin within and without! Ah, I could not say to you, "Pray," not even to you saints, unless it were a throne of grace.

Much less could I talk of prayer to you sinners. But now I will say this to every sinner, though he thinks himself to be the worst sinner that ever lived: Cry to the Lord, and *"seek ye the LORD while he may be found"* (Isa. 55:6). A throne of grace is a place fitted for you; go to your knees. By simple faith go to the Savior, for He, He it is who is the throne of grace. It is in Him that God is able to dispense grace to the most guilty of mankind. Blessed be God, neither the faults of the prayer nor those of the suppliant will shut out our petitions from the God who delights in broken and contrite hearts.

Desires Interpreted

If it is a throne of grace, then the desires of the pleader will be interpreted. If I cannot find words in which to utter my desires, God in His grace will read my desires without the words. He takes the meaning of His saints, the meaning of their groans. A throne that was not gracious would not trouble itself to make out our petitions. But God, the infinitely gracious One, will dive into the soul of our desires, and He will read there what we cannot speak with the tongue.

Have you ever seen a parent, when his child is trying to say something to him and he knows very well what it is the little one has got to say, help him over the words and utter the syllables for him? If the little one has half-forgotten what he would say, you have seen the father suggest the word. Likewise, the ever-blessed Spirit, from the throne of grace, will help us and teach us words, no, write in our hearts the desires themselves. We have in Scripture instances where God puts words into sinners' mouths. "Take with you words," says He, "and say unto Him, 'Receive us graciously and love us freely.'" (See Hosea 14:2.)

He will put the desires and will put the expression of those desires into your spirit by His grace. He will direct your desires to the things for which you ought to seek. He will teach you your wants, though as yet you do not know them. He will suggest to you His promises so that you may be able to plead them. He will, in fact, be Alpha and Omega to your prayer just as He is to your salvation; for as salvation is from first to last of grace, so the sinner's approach to the throne of grace is of grace from first to last. What comfort this is. Will we not, my dear friends, with greater boldness draw near to this throne as we draw out the sweet meaning of these precious words, *"the throne of grace"*?

Wants Supplied

If it is a throne of grace, then all the wants of those who come to it will be supplied. The King on such a throne will not say, "You must bring to Me gifts; you must offer to Me sacrifices." It is not a throne for receiving tribute; it is a throne for dispensing gifts. Come, then, you that are poor as poverty itself. Come, you that have no merits and are destitute of virtues. Come, you that are reduced to a beggarly bankruptcy by Adam's fall and by your own transgressions. This is not the throne of majesty that supports itself by the taxation of its subjects, but it is a throne that glorifies itself by streaming forth like a fountain with floods of good things. Come, now, and receive the wine and milk that are freely given. *"Yea, come, buy wine and milk without money and without price"* (Isa. 55:1). All the petitioner's wants will be supplied because it is a throne of grace.

"The throne of grace." The word grows as I turn it over in my mind. To me it is a most delightful reflection that if I come to the throne of God in prayer, I may see a thousand defects within me, but yet there is hope. I usually feel more dissatisfied with my prayers than with anything else I do. I do not believe that it is an easy thing to pray in public so as to conduct the devotions of a large congregation rightly. We sometimes hear people commended for preaching well, but if any will be enabled to pray well, there will be an equal gift and a higher grace in it.

But, friends, suppose in our prayers there are defects of knowledge; it is a throne of grace, and our Father knows that we have need of these things. Suppose there are defects of faith; He sees our little faith and still does not reject it, small as it is. He does not in every case measure out His gifts by the degree of our faith, but by the sincerity and trueness of faith. If there are grave defects in our spirit even, and failures in the fervency or in the humility of the prayer, still, though these should not be there and are much to be deplored, grace overlooks all this and forgives all this. Still, its merciful hand is stretched out to enrich us according to our needs. Surely this ought to induce many to pray who have not prayed, and this should make us who have long been accustomed to using the consecrated art of prayer, to draw near with greater boldness than ever to the throne of grace.

Grace Enthroned

Now, regarding our text as a whole, it conveys to us the idea of grace enthroned. It is a throne, and who sits on it? It is Grace personified that is here installed in dignity. Truly, today, Grace is on a throne. In the Gospel of Jesus Christ, grace is the most predominant attribute of God.

How does it come to be so exalted? Well, grace has a throne by conquest. Grace came down to earth in the form of the Well Beloved, and it met with sin. Long and sharp was the struggle, and grace appeared to be trampled underfoot by sin. But grace at last seized sin, threw it on its own shoulders, and, though all but crushed beneath the burden, grace carried sin up to the cross and nailed it there, slew it there, and put it to death forever. Grace triumphed gloriously. For this reason, grace sits on a throne at this hour because it has conquered human sin, has borne the penalty of human guilt, and has overthrown all its enemies.

Grace, moreover, sits on the throne because it has established itself there by right. There is no injustice in the grace of God. God is as just when He forgives a believer as when He casts a sinner into hell. I believe in my own soul that there is as much and as pure a justice in the acceptance of a soul who believes in Christ as there will be in the rejection of those souls who die impenitent and are banished from Jehovah's presence. The sacrifice of Christ has enabled God to *"be just, and* [also] *the justifier of him which believeth in Jesus"* (Rom. 3:26). He who knows the word *substitution* and can give its right meaning will see that there is nothing due to punitive justice from any believer, seeing that Jesus Christ has paid all the believer's debts. Now, God would be unjust if He did not save those for whom Christ vicariously suffered, for whom His righteousness was provided, and to whom it is imputed. Grace is on the throne by conquest, and it sits there by right.

Grace is enthroned this day, friends, because Christ has finished His work and has gone into the heavens. It is enthroned in power. When we speak of its throne, we mean that it has unlimited might. Grace sits not on the footstool of God, grace stands not in the courts of God, but it sits on the throne. It is the reigning attribute; it is the king today. This is the dispensation of grace, the year of grace; grace reigns through righteousness to eternal life. We live in the era of reigning grace. *"Seeing he ever liveth to make intercession"* for the sons of men, Jesus *"is able also to save them to the uttermost that come unto God by him"* (Heb. 7:25).

Sinner, if you were to meet grace in the byway, like a traveler on his journey, I would bid you to make its acquaintance and ask its influence. If you were to meet grace as a merchant on the exchange, with treasure in his hand, I would bid you to court its friendship; it would enrich you in the hour of poverty. If you were to see grace as one of the peers of heaven, highly exalted, I would bid you to seek to get its ear. But, oh, when grace sits on the throne, I beseech you, close in with it at once. It can be no higher; it can be no greater; for it is written, *"God is love"* (1 John 4:8), which is an alias for grace. Oh, come and bow before it; come and adore the infinite mercy and grace of God. Doubt not; halt not; hesitate not. Grace is reigning; grace is God; God is love. There is *"a rainbow round about the throne...like unto an emerald"* (Rev. 4:3), the emerald of His compassion and His love. Oh, happy are the souls that can believe this and, believing it, can come at once and glorify grace by becoming instances of its power.

The Glory of Grace

Lastly, our text, if rightly read, has in it sovereignty resplendent in glory—the glory of grace. The mercy seat is a throne; though grace is there, it is still a throne. Grace does not displace sovereignty. Now, the attribute of sovereignty is very high and terrible. Its light is like a jasper stone, most precious (Rev. 21:11), and like a sapphire stone, or, as Ezekiel calls it, *"the terrible crystal"* (Ezek. 1:22). Thus says the King, the Lord of Hosts, *"I will have mercy on whom I will have mercy, and I will have compassion on whom I will have compassion"* (Rom. 9:15).

O man, who art thou that repliest against God? Shall the thing formed say to him that formed it, Why hast thou made me thus? Hath not the potter power over the clay, of the same lump to make one vessel unto honour, and another unto dishonour? (Rom. 9:20–21)

But, ah, lest any of you should be downcast by the thought of His sovereignty, I invite you to the text. It is a throne—there is sovereignty—but to every soul that knows how to pray, to every soul that by faith comes to Jesus, the true mercy seat, divine sovereignty wears no dark and terrible aspect but is full of love. It is a throne of grace. From this I gather that the sovereignty of God to a believer, to a pleader, to one who comes to God in Christ, is always exercised in pure grace. To you, to you who come to God in prayer, the sovereignty always goes like this: "I will have mercy on that sinner, though he does not deserve it, though in him there is no merit; yet because I can do as I will with my own, I will bless him, I will make him My child, and I will accept him. He will be Mine in the day when I make up My jewels."

There are yet two or three things to be discussed, and I will be done with this subject. On the throne of grace, sovereignty has placed itself under bonds of love. God will do as He wills; but, on the mercy seat, He is under bonds—bonds of His own making—for He has entered into covenant with Christ and so into covenant with His chosen. Though God is and ever must be a sovereign, He will never break His covenant, nor will He alter the word that is gone out of His mouth. He cannot be false to a covenant of His own making. When I come to God in Christ, to God on the mercy seat, I need not imagine that by any act of sovereignty God will set aside His covenant. That cannot be; it is impossible.

Moreover, on the throne of grace, God is again bound to us by His promises. The covenant contains in it many gracious promises, exceedingly great and precious. *"Ask, and it shall be given you; seek, and ye shall find; knock, and it shall be opened unto you"* (Matt. 7:7). Until God had said that word or a word to that effect, it was at His own option to hear prayer or not, but it is not so now. For now, if it is true prayer offered through Jesus Christ, His truth binds Him to hear it. A man may be perfectly free, but the moment he makes a promise, he is not free to break it; and the everlasting God does not want to break His promise. He delights to fulfill it. He has declared that all His promises are *"yea"* and *"amen"* (2 Cor. 1:20) in Christ Jesus. For our consolation, when we survey God under the high and awesome aspect of His sovereignty, we have this to reflect on: He is under covenant bonds of promise to be faithful to the souls that seek Him. His throne must be a throne of grace to His people.

Once more, and the sweetest thought of all, every covenant promise has been endorsed and sealed with blood, and far be it from the everlasting God to pour scorn upon the blood of His dear Son. When a king has given a charter to a city, he may have been absolute before, and there may have been nothing to check his prerogatives; however, when the city has its charter, then it pleads its rights before the king.

Even thus, God has given to His people a charter of untold blessings, bestowing upon them the sure mercies of David. Very much of the validity of a charter depends on the signature and the seal, and, my friends, how sure is the charter of covenant grace! The signature is the handwriting of God Himself, and the seal is the blood of the Only Begotten. The covenant is ratified with blood, the blood of His own dear Son. It is not possible that we can plead in vain with God when we plead the blood-sealed covenant, ordered in all things and sure. *"Heaven and earth shall pass away"* (Matt. 24:35), but the power of the blood of Jesus can never fail with God. It speaks when we are silent, and it prevails when we are defeated. *"Better things than that of Abel"* (Heb. 12:24) does it ask for, and its cry is heard. Let us come boldly, for we bear the promise in our hearts. When we feel alarmed because of the sovereignty of God, let us cheerfully sing:

> The gospel bears my spirit up,
>   A faithful and unchanging God
> Lays the foundation for my hope
>   In oaths, and promises, and blood.

May God the Holy Spirit help us to use rightly from this time forward *"the throne of grace."* Amen.

Chapter Six

Exclamatory Prayer

So I prayed to the God of heaven.
—Nehemiah 2:4

As we see in the reading of the Scripture, Nehemiah had made inquiry as to the state of the city of Jerusalem, and the tidings he heard caused him bitter grief. *"Why should not my countenance be sad,"* he said, *"when the city, the place of my fathers' sepulchres, lieth waste, and the gates thereof are consumed with fire?"* (Neh. 2:3). He could not endure that it should be a mere ruinous heap—that city which was once *"beautiful for situation, the joy of the whole earth"* (Ps. 48:2).

Laying the matter to heart, he did not begin to speak to other people about what they would do, nor did he draw up a wonderful scheme about what might be done if so many thousand people joined in the enterprise. It occurred to him that he would do something himself. This is just the way that practical men start a matter. The unpractical will plan, arrange, and speculate about what may be done, but the genuine, thorough-going lover of Zion puts this question to himself: "What can you do? Nehemiah, what can you yourself do? Come, it has to be done, and you are the man to do it—at least, to do your share. What can you do?"

Coming so far, he resolved to set apart a time for prayer. He never had it out of his mind for nearly four months. Day and night Jerusalem seemed written on his heart, as if the name were painted on his eyeballs. He could only see Jerusalem. When he slept, he dreamed about Jerusalem. When he woke, the first thought was, "Poor Jerusalem!" And before he fell asleep again, his evening prayer was for the ruined walls of Jerusalem. The man of one thing, you know, is a formidable man; and when one single passion has absorbed the whole of his manhood, something will be sure to come of it. Depend upon that. The desire of his heart will develop into some open demonstration, especially if he talks the matter over before God in prayer. Something did come of this. Before long Nehemiah had an opportunity.

Men of God, if you want to serve God and cannot find the favorable occasion, wait awhile in prayer, and your opportunity will break on your path like a sunbeam. There was never a true and valiant heart that failed to find a fitting sphere somewhere or other in His service. Every diligent laborer is needed in some part of His vineyard. You may have to linger; you may seem as if you stood in the market idle because the Master would not engage you; but wait there in prayer and with your heart boiling over with a warm purpose, and your chance will come. The hour will need its man, and if you are ready, you, as a man, will not be without your hour.

God sent Nehemiah an opportunity. That opportunity came, it is true, in a way that he could not have expected. It came through his own sadness of heart. This matter preyed upon his mind until he began to look exceedingly unhappy. I cannot tell whether others remarked it, but the king whom he served, when he went into court with the royal goblet, noticed the distress on the cupbearer's countenance. He said to him, *"Why is thy countenance sad, seeing thou art not sick? this is nothing else but sorrow of heart"* (Neh. 2:2). Nehemiah little knew that his prayer was making the occasion for him. The prayer was registering itself upon his face. His fasting was making its marks upon his visage, and although he did not know it, he was in that way preparing the opportunity for himself when he went in before the king.

But, you see, when the opportunity did come, there was trouble with it, for he said, *"I was very sore afraid"* (Neh. 2:2). Thereupon the king asked him what he really wished; by the manner of the question he seemed to imply an assurance that he meant to help him. And here, we are somewhat surprised to find that, instead of promptly answering the king (the answer is not given immediately), an incident occurs, a fact is related. Though he was a man who had lately given himself up to prayer and fasting, this little parenthetical remark was made: *"So I prayed to the God of heaven."*

My preamble leads up to this parenthetical remark. Upon this prayer I propose to expound. Three thoughts occur to me here, on each of which I intend to enlarge: the fact that Nehemiah did pray just then, the manner of his prayer, and the excellent kind of prayer he used.

The Fact That Nehemiah Prayed

The fact that Nehemiah prayed challenges attention. He had been asked a question by his sovereign. The proper thing you would suppose was to answer it. Not so. Before he answered, he *"prayed to the God of heaven."* I do not suppose the king noticed the pause. Probably the interval was not long enough to be noticed, but it was long enough for God to notice it, long enough for Nehemiah to have sought and have obtained guidance from God as to how to frame his answer to the king. Are you not surprised to find a man of God having time to pray to God between a question and an answer? Yet Nehemiah found that time.

We are the more astonished at his praying because he was so evidently perturbed in mind, for, according to the second verse, he was *"very sore afraid."* When you are fluttered and put out, you may forget to pray. Do you not, some of you, account it a valid excuse for omitting your ordinary devotion? Nehemiah, however, felt that if he were alarmed, it was a reason for praying, not for forgetting to pray. So habitually was he in communion with God that as soon as he found himself in a dilemma, he flew away to God, just as the dove would fly to hide herself in the clefts of the rock.

His prayer was the more remarkable on this occasion because he must have felt very eager about his object. The king asked him what he wanted, and his whole heart was set upon building up Jerusalem. Are you not surprised that he did not at once say, "O king, live forever. I long to build up Jerusalem's walls. Give me all the help you can"? But no, eager as he was to pounce upon the desired object, he withdrew his hand until it is said, *"So I prayed to the God of heaven."*

I confess I admire him. I desire also to imitate him. I desire that every Christian's heart might have just that holy caution that did not permit him to be too hasty. Prayer and provisions hinder no man's journey. Certainly, when the desire of our heart is close before us, we are anxious to seize it; but we will be all the surer of getting the bird we spy in the bush into our hands if we quietly pause, lift up our hearts, and pray to the God of heaven.

It is all the more surprising that he should have deliberately prayed just then because he had already been praying for the past three or four months concerning the identical matter. Some of us would have said, "That is the thing I have been praying for; now all I have got to do is to take it and use it. Why pray any more? After all my midnight tears and daily cries, after setting myself apart by fasting to cry to the God of heaven, after such an anxious conference, surely at last the answer has come. What is to be done except to take the good that God provides me with and rejoice in it?" But no, you will always find that the man who has prayed much is the man to pray more. *"For unto every one that hath shall be given, and he shall have abundance"* (Matt. 25:29). If only you know the sweet art of prayer, you are the one who will be often engaged in it. If you are familiar with the mercy seat, you will constantly visit it.

> For who that knows the power of prayer
> But wishes to be often there?

Thus, although Nehemiah had been praying all this while, he nevertheless must offer another petition. *"So I prayed to the God of heaven."*

One thing more is worth recollecting, namely, that he was in a king's palace, and in the palace of a heathen king, too, and he was in the very act of handing up to the king the goblet of wine. He was fulfilling his part in the state festival, I doubt not, among the glare of lamps and the glitter of gold and silver, in the midst of princes and peers of the realm. Or even if it were a private festival with the king and queen only, yet still men generally feel so impressed with the responsibility of their high position on such occasions that they are apt to forget prayer. But this devout Israelite, at such a time and in such a place, when he stood at the king's foot to hold up to him the golden goblet, refrained from answering the king's question until he had first prayed to the God of heaven.

The Manner of This Prayer

The fact that Nehemiah offered this prayer prompts us to observe the manner of his prayer. Very briefly, it was what we call exclamatory prayer, prayer which, as it were, hurls a dart and then is done. It was not the type of prayer that stands knocking at mercy's door—knock, knock, knock—but it was the concentration of many knocks into one. It was begun and completed, as it were, with one stroke. This exclamatory prayer I desire to commend to you as among the very best forms of prayer.

Notice how very short it must have been. It was introduced—slipped in, sandwiched in—between the king's question and Nehemiah's answer. As I have already said, I do not suppose it took up any time at all that was appreciable, scarcely a second. Most likely the king never observed any kind of pause or hesitation, for Nehemiah was in such a state of alarm at the question that I am persuaded he did not allow any delay or vacillation to appear, but the prayer must have been offered like an electric flash, very rapidly indeed.

In certain states of strong excitement, it is wonderful how much the mind gets through in a short time. Drowning men, when rescued and recovered, have been heard to say that while they were sinking they saw the whole panorama of their lives pass before them in a few seconds. So the mind must be capable of accomplishing much in a brief space of time. Thus, the prayer was presented like the winking of an eye. It was done intuitively, yet done it was, and it proved to be a prayer that prevailed with God.

It was a prayer of a remarkable kind. I know it was so, because Nehemiah never forgot that he did pray it. I have prayed hundreds and thousands of times and not recollected any minute detail afterwards, either as to the occasion that prompted or the emotions that excited me. But there are one or two prayers in my life that I never can forget. I have not jotted them down in a diary, but I remember when I prayed because the time was so special, the prayer was so intense, and the answer to it was so remarkable. Now, Nehemiah's prayer was never, never erased from his memory; and when these words of history were written down, he recorded this: *"So I prayed to the God of heaven."*

This Excellent Style of Praying

Now, beloved friends, I come, in the third place, to recommend to you this excellent style of praying. I will speak to the children of God mainly, to you that have faith in God. I beg you often—no, I would ask you always—to use this method of exclamatory prayer. And I pray to God, also, that some who have never prayed before would offer an exclamation to the God of heaven. I desire that a short but fervent petition, something like that of the tax collector in the temple, might go up from you: *"God be merciful to me a sinner"* (Luke 18:13).

To deal with this matter practically, then, it is the duty and privilege of every Christian to have set times of prayer. I cannot understand a man's keeping up the vitality of godliness unless he regularly retires for prayer, morning and evening, at the very least. Daniel prayed three times a day, and David says, *"Seven times a day do I praise thee"* (Ps. 119:164). It is good for your hearts, good for your memory, good for your moral consistency, that you hedge about certain portions of time and say, "These belong to God. I will do business with God at such and such a time and will try to be as punctual to my hours with Him as I would be if I made an engagement to meet a friend."

When Sir Thomas Abney was Lord Mayor of London, a banquet somewhat troubled him, for Sir Thomas always had prayer with his family at a certain time. The difficulty was how to quit the banquet to keep up family devotions. So important did he consider it that he vacated the chair, saying to a person nearby that he had a special engagement with a dear friend that he must keep. And he did keep it, and he returned again to his place, none of the company being the wiser, but he himself being all the better for observing his usual habit of worship.

Mrs. Rowe used to say that when her time came for prayer, she would not give it up if the apostle Paul were preaching. No, she said, if all the twelve apostles were there and could be heard at no other time, she would not absent herself from her prayer closet when the set time came around.

But now, having urged the importance of such habitual piety, I want to impress on you the value of another sort of prayer, namely, the short, brief, quick, frequent exclamations of which Nehemiah gives us a specimen. And I recommend this because it hinders no engagement and occupies no time. You may be measuring off your calicoes or buying your groceries, or you may be adding up an account, and between the items you may say, "Lord, help me." You may breathe a prayer to heaven and say, "Lord, keep me." It will take no time.

Exclamatory prayers are of great advantage to people who are hard-pressed in business, because such prayers will not, in the slightest degree, incapacitate them from attending to the business at hand. It requires you to go to no particular place. You can stand where you are, ride in a cab, walk along the streets, be a sawyer in a sawmill, and yet pray just as well such prayers as these. No altar, no church, no so-called sacred place is needed; but wherever you are, just such a little prayer as that will reach the ear of God and win a blessing.

Such a prayer as that can be offered anywhere, under any circumstances. On the land or on the sea, in sickness or in health, amid losses or gains, great reverses or good returns, still might a man breathe his soul in short, quick sentences to God. The advantage of such a way of praying is that you can pray often and pray always. The habit of prayer is blessed, but the spirit of prayer is better. It is the spirit of prayer that is the mother of these exclamations; therefore do I like them because she is a plentiful mother. Many times in a day, we may speak with the Lord our God.

Such prayer may be suggested by all sorts of surroundings. I recollect a poor man once paying me a compliment that I highly valued at the time. He was lying in a hospital, and when I called to see him, he said, "I heard you for some years, and now whatever I look at seems to remind me of something or other that you said, and it comes back to me as fresh as when I first heard it."

Well, now, he that knows how to pray exclamatory prayers will find everything around him helping him to the sacred habit. Is it a beautiful landscape? Say, "Blessed be God, who has strewn these treasures of form and color through the world, to cheer my sight and gladden my heart." Are you in doleful darkness, and is it a foggy day? Say, "Lighten my darkness, O Lord." Are you in the midst of company? You will be reminded to pray, "Lord, *'keep the door of my lips'* (Ps. 141:3)." Are you quite alone? Then you can say, "Let me not be alone, but be with me, Father." The putting on of your clothes, the sitting at the breakfast table, the getting into the vehicle, the walking the streets, the opening of your ledger, the closing of your window, everything may suggest such prayer as that which I am trying to describe, if you are only in the right frame of mind for offering it.

These prayers are commendable because they are truly spiritual. Wordy prayers may also be windy prayers. There is much of praying from books that has nothing whatever to recommend it. How much benefit would a manual of French conversation be to anyone traveling in France without a knowledge of the language? That is how much good a manual of prayers is to a poor soul who does not know how to ask our heavenly Father for a boon or benefit that he needs. A manual, a handbook, indeed! Pray with your heart, not with your hands. Or, if you would lift hands in prayer, let them be your own hands, not another man's. The prayers that come leaping out of the soul—the gust of strong emotion, fervent desire, lively faith—these are the truly spiritual prayers; and no prayers but spiritual prayers will God accept.

This kind of prayer is free from any suspicion that it is prompted by the corrupt motive of being offered to please men. They cannot say that the secret exclamations of our soul are presented with any view to our own praise, for no man knows that we are praying at all; therefore do I recommend such prayers to you and hope that you may abound in them.

There have been hypocrites that have prayed by the hour. I doubt not that there are hypocrites as regular at their devotions as the angels are before the throne of God, and yet there is no life, no spirit, and no acceptance in their pretentious homage. But he who exclaims—whose heart talks with God—he is no hypocrite. There is a reality and force and life in his prayers. If I see sparks come out of a chimney, I know there is a fire inside somewhere, and exclamatory prayers are like the sparks that fly from a soul that is filled with burning coals of love to Jesus Christ.

Short, exclamatory prayers are of great use to us, dear friends. Oftentimes they check us. Bad-tempered people, if you would always pray just a little before you let angry expressions fly from your lips, why, many times you would not say those naughty words at all. A good woman was advised to take a glass of water and hold some of it in her mouth five minutes before she scolded her husband. I dare say it was not a bad recipe; but if, instead of practicing that little eccentricity, she would just breathe a short prayer to God, it would certainly be more effective and far more scriptural. I can recommend it as a valuable prescription for the hasty and the irritable, for all who are quick to take offense and slow to forgive insult or injury. When you are about to close a business deal, about the propriety of which you have a little doubt or a positive scruple, such a prayer as, "Guide me, good Lord" would often keep you back from doing what you would afterwards regret.

The habit of offering these brief prayers would also check your confidence in yourself. It would show your dependence upon God. It would keep you from getting worldly. It would be like sweet perfume burnt in the chamber of your soul to keep away the fever of the world from your heart. I can strongly recommend these short, sweet, blessed prayers. May the Holy Spirit give them to you!

Besides, they actually bring us blessings from heaven. Take the case of Eliezer, the servant of Abraham. (See Genesis 24:12–14.) Look at the case of Jacob when he said, even in dying, *"I have waited for thy salvation, O LORD"* (Gen. 49:18). Moses offered prayers on occasions when we do not read that he prayed at all at the time, yet God said to him, *"Wherefore criest thou unto me?"* (Exod. 14:15). David frequently presented exclamations. These prayers were all successful with the Most High. Therefore abound in them, for God loves to encourage and to answer them.

I could thus keep on recommending exclamatory prayer, but I will say one more thing in its favor. I believe it is very suitable to some people of a peculiar temperament who could not pray for a long time to save their lives. Their minds are rapid and quick. Well, dear friends, time is not an element in the business. God does not hear us because of the length of our prayer, but because of the sincerity of it. Prayer is not to be measured by the yard or weighed by the pound. It is the might and force of it, the truth and reality of it, the energy and the intensity of it. You who are either of so little a mind or of so quick a mind that you cannot use many words or continue long to think of one thing, it should be to your comfort that exclamatory prayers are acceptable.

And it may be, dear friend, that you are in a condition of body in which you cannot pray any other way. A headache such as some people are frequently affected with for the major part of their lives—a state of body that the physician can explain to you—might prevent the mind from concentrating itself long on one subject. Then, it is refreshing to be able again and again and again—fifty or a hundred times a day—to address one's self to God in short, quick sentences, the soul being all on fire. This is a blessed style of praying.

Now, I will conclude by just mentioning a few of the times when I think we ought to resort to this practice of exclamatory prayer. Mr.

Rowland Hill was a remarkable man for the depth of his piety; but when I asked at Wotton-under-Edge for his study, though I rather pressed the question, I did not obtain a satisfactory reply. At length the good minister said, "The fact is, we never found any. Mr. Hill used to study in the garden, in the parlor, in the bedroom, in the streets, in the woods, anywhere." I asked where he retired for prayer. They said that they supposed it was in his chamber but that he was always praying, that it did not matter where he was, the good old man was always praying. It seemed as if his whole life, though he spent it in the midst of his fellowmen doing good, was passed in perpetual prayer. He had been known to stand on Black Friars' Road, with his hands under his coattails, looking in a shop window, and if you listened, you might soon perceive that he was breathing out his soul before God. He was in a constant state of prayer. I believe it is the best condition in which a man can be—praying always, praying without ceasing, always drawing near to God with these exclamations.

But, if I must give you a selection of suitable times, I will mention such as these. Whenever you have a great joy, cry, "Lord, make this a real blessing to me." Do not exclaim with others, "Am I not lucky?" but say,

"Lord, give me more grace and more gratitude, now that You multiply Your favors." When you have got any arduous undertaking at hand or a heavy piece of business, do not touch it until you have breathed your soul out in a short prayer. When you have a difficulty before you and you are seriously perplexed, when business has got into a tangle or a confusion that you cannot unravel or arrange, breathe a prayer. It need not occupy a minute, but it is wonderful how many snarls come loose after just a word of prayer.

Are the children particularly troublesome to you, good woman? Does it seem as if your patience were almost worn out with worry? Now is the time for an exclamatory prayer. You will manage them all the better, and you will bear with their naughty tempers all the more quietly. At any rate, your own mind will be the less ruffled.

Do you think that there is a temptation before you? Do you begin to suspect that somebody is plotting against you? Now offer a prayer, *"Lead me in a plain path, because of mine enemies"* (Ps. 27:11).

Are you at work at the bench or in a shop or in a warehouse where lewd conversation and shameful blasphemies assail your ears? Now lift up a short prayer. Have you noticed some sin that grieves you? Let it move you to prayer. These things ought to remind you to pray. I believe the Devil would not let people swear so much if Christian people always prayed every time they heard an oath. He would then see it did not pay. Their blasphemies might somewhat be hushed if they provoked us to supplication.

Do you feel your own heart going off track? Does sin begin to fascinate you? Now utter a prayer—a warm, earnest, passionate cry—"Lord, *'hold thou me up'*" (Ps. 119:117). Did you see something with your eye, and did that eye infect your heart? Do you feel as if your *"feet were almost gone;* [and your] *steps had well nigh slipped"* (Ps. 73:2)? Now offer a prayer: "Hold me, Lord, by my right hand." Has something quite unlooked-for happened? Has a friend treated you badly? Then, like David say, *"LORD, I pray thee, turn the counsel of Ahithophel into foolishness"* (2 Sam. 15:31). Breathe a prayer now.

Are you eager to do some good? Be sure to have a prayer over it. Do you mean to speak to that young man as he goes out of the church tonight about his soul? Pray first, Christian. Do you mean to address yourself to the members of your class and write them a letter this week about their spiritual welfare? Pray over every line, Christian. It is always good to have praying going on while you are talking about Christ. I always find I can preach better if I can pray while I am preaching.

The mind is very remarkable in its activities. It can be praying while it is studying. It can be looking up to God while it is talking to man. There can be one hand held up to receive supplies from God while the other hand is dealing out the same supplies that He is pleased to give.

Pray as long as you live. Pray when you are in great pain; the sharper the pang, the more urgent and persistent should your cry to God be. And when the shadow of death gathers around you and when strange feelings flush or chill you and plainly tell that you near the journey's end, then pray. Oh, that is a time for exclamation! Short and pithy prayers like this: *"O LORD...hide not thy face from me"* (Ps. 143:7) or this: "O God, *'Be not far from me'"* (Ps. 22:11) will doubtless suit you. *"Lord Jesus, receive my spirit"* (Acts 7:59) were the thrilling words of Stephen in his extremity. *"Father, into thy hands I commend my spirit"* were the words that your Master Himself uttered just before He bowed His head and *"gave up the ghost"* (Luke 23:46). You may well take up the same strain and imitate Him.

These thoughts and counsels are so exclusively directed to the saints and faithful friends in Christ that you will be prone to ask, "Is there not anything to be addressed to the unconverted?" Well, whatever has been expressed here may be used by them for their own benefit. But, let me address myself to you, my dear friends, as pointedly as I can. Though you are not saved, you must not say, "I cannot pray." Why, if prayer is simply thus, what excuse can you have for neglecting it? It needs no measurable space of time. Such prayers as these God will hear; and you have, all of you, the ability and opportunity to think and to express them. All you need to pray these prayers is that elementary faith in God that believes *"that he is, and that he is a rewarder of them that diligently seek him"* (Heb. 11:6). Cornelius had, I suppose, gone about as far as this when he was admonished by the angel to send for Peter, who preached to him peace by Jesus Christ to the conversion of his soul.

Is there such a strange being as a man or woman that never prays? How should I reason with you? May I steal a passage from a living poet who, though he has contributed nothing to our hymn books, hums a note so suited to my purpose and so pleasant to my ear that I like to quote it?

More things are wrought by prayer
Than this world dreams of. Wherefore let thy
    voice
Rise like a fountain, flowing night and day:
For what are men better than sheep or goats,
That nourish a blind life within the brain,
If, knowing God, they lift not hands of prayer,
Both for themselves and those who call them
    friend?
For so the whole round world is every way
Bound by gold chains about the feet of God.

I do not suspect there is a creature who never prays, because people generally pray to somebody or other. The man who never prays to God such prayers as he ought, prays to God such prayers as he ought not. It is an awful thing when a man asks God to damn him, and yet there are people who do that. Suppose He were to hear you; He is a prayer-hearing God.

If I address one profane swearer, I would like to put this matter clearly to him. Were the Almighty to hear you—if your eyes were blinded and your tongue were struck dumb while you were uttering a wild curse—how would you bear the sudden judgment on your impious speech? If some of those prayers of yours were answered for yourself and if some that you have offered in your passion for your wife and for your children were fulfilled to their hurt and your distraction, what an awful thing it would be.

Well, God does answer prayer, and one of these days He may answer your prayers to your shame and everlasting confusion. Would it not be well to pray now, "Lord, have mercy upon me. Lord, save me. Lord, change my heart. Lord, give me faith to believe in Christ. Lord, give me now an interest in the precious blood of Jesus. Lord, save me now"? Will not each one of you breathe such a prayer as that? May the Holy Spirit lead you to do so.

If you once begin to pray rightly, I am not afraid that you will ever cease, for there is something that holds the soul fast in real prayer. Sham prayers—what is the good of them? But real heart pleading—the soul talking with God—when it once begins, will never cease. You will have to pray until you exchange prayer for praise and until you go from the mercy seat below to the throne of God above.

May God bless you all. All of you, I say, all who are my kindred in Christ and all for whose salvation I yearn. God bless you all and every one, for our dear Redeemer's sake. Amen.